Thomas Wm. Madron is Manager of Academic Computing Services at North Texas State University in Denton. In addition to frequent appearances on local radio and television talk shows, he has written several articles in leading microcomputer journals.

Thomas Wm. Madron

MICRO-COMPUTERS IN LARGE ORGANIZATIONS

A SPECTRUM BOOK

Prentice–Hall, Inc., Englewood Cliffs, New Jersey 07632

Library of Congress Cataloging in Publication Data

Madron, Thomas William, (date)
  Microcomputers in large organizations.

  "A Spectrum Book."
  Bibliography: p.
  Includes Index.
  1. Microcomputers. I. Title.
  QA76.5.M18765 1983   001.64   82-14977
  ISBN 0-13-580795-6
  ISBN 0-13-580787-5 (pbk.)

This book is available at a special discount when ordered in
bulk quantities. Contact Prentice-Hall, Inc., General
Publishing Division, Special Sales, Englewood Cliffs, N.J. 07632.

1 2 3 4 5 6 7 8 9 10

ISBN 0-13-580795-6

ISBN 0-13-580787-5 {PBK.}

Prentice-Hall International, Inc., *London*
Prentice-Hall of Australia Pty. Limited, *Sydney*
Prentice-Hall Canada Inc., *Toronto*
Prentice-Hall of India Private Limited, *New Delhi*
Prentice-Hall of Japan, Inc., *Tokyo*
Prentice-Hall of Southeast Asia Pte. Ltd., *Singapore*
Whitehall Books Limited, *Wellington, New Zealand*
Editora Prentice-Hall do Brasil Ltda., *Rio de Janeiro*

Contents

Preface

Microcomputers in Large Organizations is designed to provide some insights into how microcomputers (or personal computers) are being used in large organizations, how they will be used during the eighties, and what we might expect of them through the eighties and into the nineties. In describing how they are and how they can be used, we will also be concerned with the role microcomputing can play in the overall data processing plans of the organization. Proper planning, especially in large organizations, is essential for micros to be used well. In addition, the attempt is made (successfully, we hope) to show how we should approach the use of micros in an integrated fashion, especially in their potential use as manager's work stations. The design considerations for a manager's work station should be useful to anyone wishing to use microcomputers.

In preparing this book I must extend thanks to several people and groups. In particular, I wish to express my thanks to Dr. Beverly Madron (my wife) and to Ms. Claudia Putnam (my colleague and assistant) for their critical reading and correction of the manuscript. In addition, I wish to thank Ms. Carolyn Marks (a friend and former colleague) for supplying the information concerning the FMC Corporation, used in the case study in Chapter 6 (and, of course, FMC Corporation for allowing it to be used). Finally, the Dallas Chapter of DPMA assisted me greatly (especially in allowing me to use their membership list) in doing the survey reported in Chapter 6. All of these people and organizations contributed to the strengths of the book. Only I am responsible for any weaknesses.

Microcomputing in the 1980s

Through the late 1980s microcomputers will become as common in large organizations as calculators and perhaps even as telephones. Certainly if the major manufacturers of microcomputers have anything to say about it, businesses —from the Fortune 500 companies to smaller organizations — will be acquiring microcomputers in large numbers. This book is about the uses to which microcomputers can be put in institutions that already may have large-scale computing available —organizations in business, industry, government, and education. The big market for micros in the mid-1980s is with the giants, although it is likely that growth in personal computing will occur as well.

MICROCOMPUTERS AND MICROCOMPUTING

Why should large organizations want to acquire microcomputers? The answer to that question, which is a major focus of this book, is threefold: (1)

1

the capabilities of micros, (2) the demands of large organizations on the time of their employees (especially at the managerial level), and (3) the human factors associated with the large-scale work environment. In some respects micros hold out the promise of making Space Age technology available for even the most mundane tasks. Alternatively, micros sometimes can make even routine work more interesting to complete. An old (albeit sexist) saying notes that the "difference between men and boys is the price of their toys." Are micros the new wave of technology for the white collar worker, or are they simply a passing fad for managers in need of some sophisticated recreation?

The "microcomputer" or "personal computer" acquired its name from its physically small size and (by present-day standards) somewhat limited memory size and speed. It used to be common to talk about "mainframe computers" (really large ones), "minicomputers" (middle-sized ones), and now "microcomputers" or "personal computers." The distinctions were based on the amount of available memory, the speed by which instructions could be executed, physical size, and other factors. By the early 1980s, however, such distinctions were often more apparent than real. When we see a very large machine (such as an IBM 3033 or 3081 or a National [Semiconductor] AS/7000 or AS/9000, for example), we know it is a mainframe computer because of its physical size and in IBM's case, the need for plumbing to keep the machine cool.

Yet today's microcomputers have as much or more capacity and capability than the most commonly used machines of the late 1960s or early 1970s. And herein lies one of the attractions for organizations and their managers beset by the need to produce with greater efficiency and effectiveness. For a modest price it is possible to have on one's desk a computer capable of assisting with many common office chores: word processing, financial planning and modeling, mathematical calculations, note taking, and a multitude of other tasks. (And during coffee breaks they can become recreational machines.)

The "personal" aspect of personal computers cannot be overemphasized. One of the primary reasons microcomputers have such significant appeal is that they are a personal or individual tool, not one shared by many. Consequently they are not subject to the vagaries of a large number of users and support staffs. In a way, personal also means private. The person using a microcomputer can test out ideas without risking his/her "image" in the organization. In this book the terms "personal computer" and "microcomputer" will be used synonymously. One collective objective of any large organization is to make its staff more productive, and one way to make the people in the organization more productive is to provide them with better tools. Especially for the white collar work force, one of the major productivity tools of the 1980s is the personal computer. This point of view has already become accepted in many major organizations and will expand to include others during the decade.

Microcomputers first made their way into the computer marketplace in the mid to late 1970s with the development of central processing units (CPUs) condensed into a single integrated circuit chip in a package smaller than a single domino. The CPU in any computer is the real "brain" of the machine — it processes the instructions or programs. Although the early micros were both small and relatively inexpensive compared to mini and mainframe computers, it was not until the late 1970s that the devices were available at a price that made them accessible to a large consumer market. Indeed, the primary focus of early marketing efforts was to hobbyists, later to the general public and to small businesses, and only in the early 1980s to large organizations. When Radio Shack (Tandy) with its TRS-80 series, Apple Computers, Inc. with the Apple computer, and Commodore with the PET (and its successors) made personal computers readily available at consumer prices, the microcomputer market exploded.

Like their larger relatives (the minis and the mainframes), micros are general purpose computers that are instructed in their tasks through programs written in a variety of computer languages. Most of the major high level languages familiar to users or larger systems are available: BASIC, FORTRAN, COBOL, PL/I, and others. In addition, other languages, such as Pascal, are becoming widespread in the 1980s. For many applications, however, it is not necessary for an individual to become a programmer, because there are thousands of "off-the-shelf" programs on the market. In fact, the microcomputer manufacturers have (somewhat unwittingly) spawned an extensive support industry replete with software vendors, and major publishers vying for the software market. Software is a catch-all phrase that refers to the programs necessary to make the computers (hardware) and their "peripherals" (disks, tapes, printers, etc.) do appropriate tasks. In many respects the advent of micros could be to the latter quarter of the twentieth century what Gutenburg's invention of movable type was to the fifteenth.

Microcomputer Manufacturers
Target Large Users

By the early 1980s (1980–1981) a few hundred thousand microcomputers had been sold, most of them by Radio Shack, Apple, or Commodore, although there was a fairly large number of other (though smaller) manufacturers. Moreover, by mid-1981 it was clear that some of the industry giants were getting into the microcomputer business, such as IBM, Xerox, Hewlett-Packard, and others. By 1981 it was also clear, as Jean Bozman (*Infosystems News*, August 24, 1981, p. 6) noted, that "personal computers, which used to be carried into Fortune 1000 companies at night by overworked department managers, are now arriving through the front door." It is the large-scale market, major corporations, educational institutions, and governmental agencies, which seem to have been targeted for the mid-1980s by the microcomputer manufacturers.

Early in 1981 it became apparent that micro manufacturers were setting their sights on large-scale users when Radio Shack introduced bisynchronous communications support for its TRS-80 Model II (the larger version of its micro). Bisynchronous communications refers to the way in which communications can be established between a large computer (typically an IBM computer) and a terminal. The communications equipment needed for bisynchronous support is not usually appropriate (because of cost) for personal communications and is used almost exclusively on large IBM machines in big organizations. When it became known that such support was on its way, there were commentaries in publications serving the market that Tandy (Radio Shack) was making a big mistake.

Yet it is that same market in which others seem particularly interested. *80 Microcomputing* in its August 1981 issue reported that "Tandy/Radio Shack, Fort Worth, TX, is trying to beat IBM to the punch by making the TRS-80 Model II compatible with IBM equipment before the industry giant brings out its own micros." The bisynchronous communications support announced by Tandy provides the TRS-80 Model II the capability of communicating with large IBM mainframes in the same way used by IBM's own terminals. Moreover, when IBM announced its personal computer in September 1981, it also announced its intent to provide bisynchronous software.

When these announcements were made, not all parts of the industry were reading the potential market the same way. Rory J. O'Connor reported in the June 1, 1981 issue of *Computer Business News* that "Outside observers . . . told CBN the case for IBM compatibility on the TRS-80 is weak and that only certain large-volume users of the equipment would ever need the software."

One such outside observer was a spokesperson for Galactic Software, Inc., a publisher of computer games and other software aimed at the personal use of micros by individuals. Bob Snapp of Snapp Inc. commented that the "market for these IBM products is quite limited. At most, 2 percent of prospective TRS-80 users are at all interested." Such points of view tend to be somewhat shortsighted and do not reflect what is actually taking place in larger organizations. They do not take into account what is likely to happen over the remainder of the 1980s. Some large manufacturers, such as Texas Instruments with its 99/4 microcomputer, misread even the earlier market for micros. Although Texas Instrument could have produced an excellent product, it actually produced a computer that was only marginally better than a game machine. Texas Instruments announced its own business-oriented machine in October 1981.

By late summer of 1981, however, industry news media were reporting quite different perspectives from those previously put forth on the impact of micros in larger organizations and were beginning to report the reasoning of the manufacturers. Jean Bozman in August 1981 reported that both IBM and Xerox, with the advent of their microcomputer systems, were gearing up for a major run at the Fortune 1000 companies. She quoted John Shirley, director of marketing for Radio Shack, as saying that "we've been pursuing an active program of selling to the major companies for the last nine months." As of August 1981, Shirley indicated that 190 of the Fortune 1000 had signed major accounts for personal computers. Apple Computers said that "one-third of all its sales go to business, and half of that to Fortune 1000 companies." Since (at that time) Apple had about a 23 percent share of the market, that meant 7.3 percent of that total market share was buying Apples for business and that 3.8 percent of the total market was in sales to Fortune 1000 companies.

Clearly the perception of the market by groups such as Snapp Inc. and Galactic Software, Inc. was wrong. Snapp's judgment that only about 2 percent of potential buyers (for the TRS-80 market) might be interested in such things as IBM communications capability was quite likely incorrect. At least the Fortune 1000 companies (or a great majority of them) would have such a potential interest, as evidenced by Tandy's sales effort. The Fortune 1000 companies along with other, not quite so large businesses, educational institutions, and governmental agencies represent a potential market for microcomputers numbering in sales of anywhere from hundreds to thousands for any given agency. Think what the market is if micros become as pervasive as typewriters in the offices of the future. Bozman quoted a spokesperson for Ohio Scientific as saying that "you're going to find a personal computer on the desktops of the entire white collar work force, right along with the telephone as a standard piece of equipment."

Planning for Microcomputing

The microcomputer manufacturers are clearly planning for large-scale use of microcomputers by big organizations. But are the organizations themselves planning for their use? The public sector of the economy, including educational and governmental agencies, often receives criticism for its inability to plan properly for the deployment of new technologies as they become available. Granted it is often difficult, especially when dealing with computer technology, for agencies, whether public or private, to keep pace with the rapid rate of growth and change in the technology itself. Obsolescence occurs not as extensively from marketing strategies of vendors (although this happens, of course) as from new technological developments. It is possible, however, to do some short-term and medium range planning. The microcomputer manufacturers are obviously doing such planning and forecasting — but are the rest of us?

Large organizations — in business, industry, education, and government — are acquiring microcomputers whether there is planning or not. One well-known university, for example, found that it had acquired some 350 microcomputers and decided it might be time to do some planning for future growth. Precisely the same thing is happening in the private sector. And micros may not even show up on anyone's inventory control list as "computer" equipment but rather as office equipment or perhaps "terminals." Institutions will acquire micros because they are inexpensive enough to be imbedded within a variety of budgetary nooks and crannies. The issue is not whether large organizations will acquire micros but whether they will be acquired and deployed in a coherently planned manner or by a policy of neglect.

When the background work for this book was done, a survey of microcomputer use of 136 individuals was made in Dallas, Texas. The results of the survey are discussed extensively in Chapter 6. Of that number, 83.1 percent (113) represented large organizations; 54.9 percent of the people from large organizations had some micros. Only one person claimed to be from an organization with any plan in place for future deployment and use, although several said they planned to buy more.

Perhaps part of the reason that so little planning is taking place is that there is sometimes debate, at other times outright war, between the institutional or corporate DP center management and those wishing to acquire micros. The typical buyer of microcomputers in a larger organization is likely to be a member of middle management, sometimes attempting to bypass programmers, operators, and the cost and red tape involved in using central computing facilities. Data processing managers, on the other hand, frequently know little about micros and are concerned with mainframes, time sharing, and massive data networks. These large-scale facilities require planning for efficient access across a large organization. Jason Birmingham, in "Computer Crossfire in the Corporate World" (*Personal Computing,* November 1981, pp. 23–28), argues that not only is an internal corporate war shaping up, but that right is on the side of the corporate personal computer user.

Although it is unfortunately true that many DP managers do resist the deployment of microcomputers, it is also true that the institutional DP center must be involved in the deployment. It is unlikely that in the long run personal computers will be used entirely in a vacuum on a stand-alone basis. In fact, it is more likely that users of such equipment will quickly learn that it is necessary to have access to corporate data files in order to accomplish some (if not all) the tasks for which the micro was acquired. This issue means that sooner or later a demand will arise for allowing communications access to the central system through the micro. Once the micro becomes a superintelligent terminal (one with the ability to provide a wide range of special functions for the user), it is no longer possible for an individual to operate in an environment apart from decisions made by the central computing facility.

The central computing facility also can encourage not only appropriate deployment of micros, it also can assist in distributing software developed internally so that duplication of effort is kept to reasonable levels. For example, by evaluating and standardizing communications programs for several micros, it would be possible to provide a central library (much like an internal CP/M Users Group Library or Digital Equipment Corporation's much heralded DEC Users Group (DECUS) library.

Information services, such as the Source or Compuserve, have already implemented similar software archival and distribution facilities. By providing the appropriate central facility on the mainframe computer, it would be possible for individual users to upload programs they had written, thus making them available to the entire corporate structure. Further down the line, with the assistance of the central computing facility, the network of micros easily could become nodes in a far-flung distributed processing system. In some respects this will happen anyway, once managers have a machine with sufficient intelligence to upload and download (move information from the mainframe to the micro) from other systems.

Consequences
of the Failure to Plan

As already suggested, the bottom line in any discussion of microcomputers in large organizations is that micros will be acquired whether there is planning or not. The consequences of not planning are the usual: waste, duplication, and inefficiency. More importantly, however, when micros are acquired in an unplanned manner, they will not be as well used as they might be. The lack of availability means that micros will not be used to their full capabilities, and those who need them most may have no access at all. In such a situation micros will be in the custody of those within the institution politically astute enough to acquire them. Waste, duplication, and inefficiency leads inescapably to more costly modes of organizational behavior than does responsible planning.

As most computing moves more and more to some form of online transactional use (interactive computing), we should ask what share should be processed by smaller, decentralized systems (minicomputers and microcomputers) and what share by the large central system? During the 1970s the "economy of scale" argument led to the use of very large, very centralized systems. It is equally clear that in the 1980s economy is likely to lead us to decentralized, distributed, and relatively specialized systems. Moreover, with the further use of microcomputers, especially by middle management, there will be a tendency for such users to either produce their own software in order to improve their own productivity or that of their subordinates or to buy off-the-shelf software. Both developments will likely improve the computer literacy of such managers, which ultimately will assist the planning efforts of the entire organization.

While some DP managers may resent others using micros to do tasks formerly accomplished by a central site and others may resent the intrusion of the DP manager in the life of their own local organization, the fact of the matter is that both kinds of people are interdependent in a large organization. The compromise most likely to take place is that organizational restrictions on the acquisition of micros (computing equipment outside the auspices of the central DP facility) will likely be relaxed, while at the same time central DP systems will come to take a more active role in the support and deployment of micros. If this kind of compromise does not take place, then decentralization (rather than distribution) of processing will take place, which will ultimately work to the detriment of everyone.

PROBLEMS AND OPPORTUNITIES IN THE USE OF MICROCOMPUTERS

At a time when most computing hardware is becoming less expensive (at least when measured in cost per byte of memory or disk storage or number of instructions per second), why would users who have access to large central systems wish to use micros at all? A single answer to that question is not easily or neatly phrased. However, one obvious answer is the user's independence from a central computing staff. As hardware has become less expensive, the personnel cost involved in using that hardware has become more expensive.

The issue of "independence" from a central computing facility should not be construed to mean that micros do not need professional support, especially in large organizations. A major mistake an organization could make would be to start placing micros in offices on a large scale without appropriate support personnel. Even though micros are small, useful, and full of promise and there is a considerable amount of software available "off-the-shelf", in order to make effective use of microcomputers it is still necessary to have some programming support. While some of the users of micros will learn to do much of their own programming, the objective in the acquisition of micros should not be to make middle-level managers (or others) into computer programmers. Many (perhaps most) programmers having most of their experience on large-scale systems do not have the skills necessary to handle micros with facility. Certainly they can learn, but the learning will take time. When deploying micros a large organization would be well advised to make some sort of staff (even a small one) available for assistance to those receiving the units.

Linked to the issue of independence is the insight of many users that large systems are not necessary for the kind of problems for which they might use computers. A case in point is the growing popularity of VISICALC (by Personal Software, Inc.) and other electronic spreadsheet programs. Similar programs exist for large mainframes but cost from $14,000 to $40,000 (according to *DATAPRO Software Directory*) as compared to $100 to $200 (depending on the implementation) for VISICALC. Moreover, in running such a program on a large system, one would find it relatively easy to amass substantial computer time charges. For the cost of a spreadsheet system on a mainframe computer (program + computer time + personnel for installation and maintenance), it would be possible to acquire several microcomputers and related software for the financial planners.

What They Can and Cannot Do

It is tempting to say that microcomputers can do anything, but that is not quite accurate. In a purely technical sense, micros perform virtually all the functions their large relatives do. Micros have more restricted memories, speed, and peripheral devices, of course, but functionally they perform the same. But their limitations dictate that micros cannot be in direct competition with large mainframes. There are simply some problems which must be solved on large, fast machines. Bear in mind, however, that the *average* microcomputer of the early 1980s was faster and had more memory and more of a variety of peripheral devices than "large" machines of the 1955–1965 (or 1970s) period. In fact, many micros routinely exceed the capacity (if not the speed) of most of the smaller machines in the old IBM 360 series. The point is, apparently to the chagrin of some DP managers, microcomputers are "real" computers capable of doing serious work in a cost-effective manner.

Just as micros cannot compete with mainframes in some data processing applications, we also should ask whether some mainframes are being used for tasks inappropriate to their size and power. The fact of the matter is that for a number of applications, using a very large mainframe is much like using a sledgehammer to drive a thumbtack, and that kind of use tends to be expensive and wasteful. Many data entry problems (including some word processing applications) are more efficiently and effectively accomplished on micros than on large machines. Instructional services such as Computer Assisted Instruction (CAI) in both education and industry probably should be done on micros rather than on large mainframes. Considerable financial analysis, planning, and modeling can be accomplished on micros with flexibility that the mainframes may find difficult to match. Some applications require the use of a dedicated micro which would be inappropriate for mainframes: security control systems (locks, badge validation, etc.), monitors for mainframe CPUs, monitors for communications systems, laboratory process control, intelligent data collection, and a host of others.

Why Large Organizations Need Microcomputers

The reasons for using microcomputers in large organizations are myriad. Part of the explanation has already been given. Considering the cost of computing, distributed across mainframes, minis, micros, communications, and programming, the most cost-effective approach to computing is through a multifaceted approach to problem-solving. But contrary to some opinion, the unplanned and leaderless use of micros is not the wave of the future — at least not for large organizations. The objectives for the use of any data processing equipment must include the need to process documents more efficiently (both textual and quantitative documents) and the need to provide appropriate information for decision-making at appropriate times. The "one big computer in the sky" concept, which dominated the 1960s and 1970s, is no longer viable in the 1980s.

One of the major functions of microcomputers in the office is making white collar workers more productive. While the productivity of American industrial (blue collar) workers has increased considerably over the decades of the sixties and seventies, there has been no concomitant improvement in the productivity of white collar workers. At least part of the answer to white collar productivity is to provide people in these occupations with the technology to do their tasks well. In many respects the microcomputer could be to the office what typewriters were to pen, pencils, and paper. And in that sense micros should be regarded as office machines rather than as computers. They are general purpose instruments that can do the tasks of a multitude of other office machines and at the same time provide capabilities not previously available to the average office worker. And if, as considerable recent literature would suggest, we see in the 1980s the distribution of offices (as well as the distribution of computing), then micros as intelligent terminals will play a central role in that development.

MICROCOMPUTERS, COMMUNICATIONS, AND DISTRIBUTED NETWORKS

Although microcomputers are being used and will continue to be used for a considerable amount of stand-alone computing, they can become superstars within a distributed computing environment. Distributed data processing (DDP) has been frequently discussed and frequently implemented. There are almost as many definitions of distributed processing as there are articles on the topic. For purposes of discussion we can manage with a relatively loose definition: distributed data processing consists of a network of computers, linked by a communications system, capable of doing tasks on a local level appropriate for a particular CPU, but using resources of one or more of the other nodes as specific tasks might demand.

Overlaid on the hardware may or may not be a distributed data base (a database conceived as being integrated but spread across machines in a DDP system). First and foremost, however, DDP does not mean *decentralized* processing. In fact, for a distributed network to work effectively there must be centralized guidance (if not outright control). A decentralized system might exist when two or more computers (of any size) are linked together with communications, but where there is no coherent attempt to view or work with the system as a whole.

In practice, of course, even in organizations where the concepts of distributed processing are given credence, the actual system probably lies somewhere between completely planned and implemented DDP and a completely decentralized system. And there are still some fairly large organizations which have only a number of local processors and do not attempt to establish communications among them. In such situations there is no effort made to construct a corporate-wide "system" of computing except, perhaps, through the issuance of printed documents. DDP networks do not need to be based on large machines at all. Xerox's ETHERNET is one example of a "local" distributed network in which each node is essentially a microcomputer or a peripheral device being used by one or more microcomputers. Within ETHERNET the micros may be called "word processors" or something else, but the intelligent machines in the system are microcomputers.

You may have noted that a new concept was slipped into the preceding paragraph: local networks. One of the distinct advantages of networking generally is that people at different points on the network can communicate cheaply and easily. These computer-based communication programs have various names and capabilities: electronic mail, message systems, bulletin boards, computer conferencing systems and more. In a 1981 speech, John W. White, assistant vice-president for Information Systems and Services at Texas Instruments, indicated that the average cost for a one-page message, communicated through the company's distributed data processing system (probably the world's largest private system), cost two to three cents. This cost should be compared to the average cost of preparing and sending a standard letter: six to seven dollars. TI's system is not a "local" DDP system — it is world-wide in character, but the concept holds. Local DDP networks can be used as easily for electronic mail as can large DDP ones.

Local DDP networks are just what the name implies: networks of relatively limited size, designed to facilitate the work of offices within a somewhat narrowly defined geographical area (although this, strictly speaking, is not essential to the concept). In a university or a large industrial complex, for example, each building might have its own local network, distributing considerable processing. Such local networks then can be connected to one another and to large central systems through "gateway" processors. If the gateways are constructed properly, it is not even necessary for the various local nets to be from the same manufacturer, or even use the same communications protocols (although this probably would be an unwise choice).

It is clear from this discussion that microcomputers play a central role in all the variations of distributed data processing. In local networks they are at the heart of the system. In large regional, national, or international systems they occupy a major place as the workstation for a local manager as an access to the larger system. When preparing a document, such as this book, for example, there is little reason for the use of a large on-line system. Yet if this were a manual to be widely distributed within the organization, one approach would be to upload the document into the DDP system and allow distribution to take place electronically.

In fact, I habitually write documents of all sorts on a micro word processing system and then upload them to the central system for printing and distribution by my secretary. My use of the central system to prepare text (thus monopolizing a port, contributing to response time problems, and the like) is minimized. Likewise, if someone on our central system sends me a message through our electronic mail system, I have the option of downloading the message to the micro or keeping it on the central system (if it deserves to be kept at all). Book publishers are developing systems by which authors may simply upload electronic text rather than sending a paper manuscript at all. In Chapter 2 we will return in a more detailed fashion to the uses of microcomputers in a network environment.

PLANNING FOR MICROCOMPUTERS

From what has been said to this point we can draw some preliminary conclusions. Microcomputers are here to stay in large organizations. Rather than being met with fear and trepidation, they should be welcomed. But there are several implicit uses to which micros may, and probably will, be applied which imply the need for planning. There are a few organizations that have already washed their hands of central planning and have established internal rules which keep the central DP organization out of the acquisition cycle for purchases under $100,000 or even more. Such a policy may prove to be premature, because it is likely that without some sort of coherent, institution-wide planning for microcomputers, the organization will not make maximum use of its machines. There are several considerations which would argue for institutional planning: communications, software, and maintenance.

Communications

Although we will delve into the substantive issues of communications in Chapter 2, they are important items to consider in the context of institutional planning. If it is the objective of a large organization to establish a corporate-wide computer communications system, then that system will impact the acquisition of microcomputers whether a local manager likes it or not. The very first issue is, of course, will the communications protocol used (the method by which communications is achieved) support micros? If the system uses only (or primarily) ASCII (American Standard Code for Information Interchange) oriented devices, then most micros can be interfaced. However, if the system is based on IBM's 3270 protocol, then only a very few micros will be able to exist within the system.

Central Planning and coordination in the acquisition of micros is essential to ensure that they will be able to be used as nodes in a distributed system. Also, it is quite likely that many middle managers will not even know when it would be useful to have a micro capable of communications. A comprehensive organizational plan, therefore, might include a requirement that any micros purchased be equipped with communications capabilities.

Software

Too frequently in many organizations decision-makers have tended to focus on the hardware available rather than on the functions to be performed by it. It is easy to fall into such a trap, especially after having seen a particularly smooth demonstration of a microcomputer using a lot of color graphics and other photogenic tricks. The first question which should be asked by a potential buyer is this: "Is software available to do the primary job for which I want a microcomputer?" If the answer to that question is "yes," then it should be asked: "For what computer?" And it is not sufficient to conclude that even when a given piece of software is available and is on a system the user likes that the buyer should be allowed to make the purchase without regard to other acquisitions within the organization.

A case in point might be the spreadsheet program VISICALC. This is available on a number of different microcomputers and appears much the same to the user in all its implementations. In an organization, however, it might be useful to be able to distribute a VISICALC model to a number of departments for review and/or revision. Because of differences among operating systems, this communication may not be easily achieved unless each unit has the same hardware.

Even when a microcomputer has been purchased because of the availability of software, sooner or later the user will discover that he/she needs something programmed. At least at the beginning it is quite likely that the individual responsible for micro will learn a little programming, but if the project is extensive, then he/she will go hunting for a programmer. Presuming that the central DP facility staff is willing to support micros at all, they cannot be expected to support a random selection of the large number of micros on the market. It would be incumbent on the institution, therefore, to limit the variety of microcomputers departments are allowed to buy. Such limitations have the further advantage that favorable purchasing contracts can often be negotiated when multiple machines from a single supplier are being acquired. In order to ensure the continued use of the micro, once acquired, it is in the organization's interest to provide some minimal level of software support.

Maintaining Microcomputers

Like all machines, microcomputers will malfunction at some time. What happens then? In a completely decentralized situation, where there is no organization-wide policy to govern maintenance, the person responsible for the machine will likely try to write a local service contract. Such contracts are available, but costs are relatively high. For one micro the cost may not seem prohibitive, but if the institution acquires a hundred or a thousand micros, then a large number of individual service contracts would be quite expensive. A better approach is to find a vendor of maintenance services that could be used organization-wide, because then very attractive maintenance prices can be negotiated. But this, like software exchange, will not work in an environment with a large number of different systems.

While it is not necessary to standardized on a single microcomputer manufacturer, it is more cost-effective to choose at least a limited number of manufacturers. Such contracts are routinely written for "dumb" terminals, why not for micros? Certainly an equivalent approach to micros can be taken, but only if there is some organization-wide policy governing not only software support for micros but hardware support as well.

LOOKING FORWARD TO MICROCOMPUTING

In this chapter we have argued that microcomputers have a major role to play in large organizations. Moreover, micros should be welcomed as a major step forward in using our technology for greater productivity. The thrust of the viewpoints put forth thus far, however, suggest that for micros to be used well, it is desirable to proceed from the perspective of an institution-wide plan for the deployment of micros rather than allowing every department to rush out and buy its own. It is doubtful that this perspective will be greeted in a universally positive manner but, policy or not, micros will be acquired.

Acquired within the context of an overall plan, micros can be joined together in local networks or as nodes in a more general distributed processing system. If acquisition is left completely in the hands of local departments, micros may be used well for a period of time, but probably will not be used well over time. In subsequent chapters we will take a closer look at micros within a communications and distributed processing environment, at actual applications in large organizations, at the experience of specific organizations with micros, and conclude with some speculation concerning the future of microcomputers in business, government, and education. If you believe that the sixties and seventies were periods of technological wonder, just wait.

Microcomputers
and Networks

In large organizations the bottom line in doing work effectively is often "communications." For that reason it is important to understand that microcomputers can be important elements in facilitating communications. By communications is meant the generic process of transferring information from one individual to another. That information may be data intelligible to people or to computers. When several devices (computers, terminals, or other devices) are connected together by an electronic communications system, then we have a computer network. In general, communications networks (such as the telephone sytem) can exist without computers, but computer networks cannot exist without communications systems.

Computer networks can be organized in a variety of ways, and some of these are described in later pages. By the early 1980s it was possible to distinguish between what has been called "local" networks and what I shall call (solely to differentiate them) "global" networks. Local networks have been described as those which "cover a limited geographical area" where every "node on the network can communicate with every other node, and . . . requires no central node or processor" (Harry J. Saal, "Local-Area Networks," *Byte*, October, 1981 pp.96–97).

In many local networks all the nodes are microcomputers. Local networks are to be distinguished from global networks in that global networks typically have at least one computer node (perhaps made up of more than a single computer) that is central to the operation of the network. The central node is at least a time-sharing minicomputer and is frequently a very large mainframe computer. In a global network microcomputers are often used as intelligent terminals within the network. Local networks may be attached to one another or may themselves be nodes in a global network. Local area networks can have radii which range from a few hundred meters to about 50 kilometers, while global networks can be extended world-wide if need be.

Why should computers — and therefore end users — be organized into networks in the first place? With computer hardware becoming less expensive and at the same time more sophisticated, the answer to this question is different in the 1980s than it was a decade or two earlier. Certainly one of the early motivating factors behind the establishment of global computer networks was that through networks many users could use expensive computer systems, thus spreading the cost of such systems over a much larger user base. It also was recognized early that within large organizations there was a need to share data as well as hardware (and software). These classic arguments are still the primary ones in favor of networking generally, whether local or global in character. When we add to the arguments noted the increasing need to share the results of our use of computers, then we see that one advantage of networks is the ability to communicate between users (with what is sometimes called electronic mail).

In an article published in 1978 ("Networks and Networking", *IASSIST Newsletter,* Vol. 2, No. 3 Summer 1978, pp. 56–68) I gave the classic arguments noted above and further contended that "although the cost of computers is falling rather rapidly, the cost of large-scale peripheral devices — devices which can be used to permanently store large quantities of data — are not decreasing in cost in any substantial fashion." The pace of technological development is such that this statement is no longer accurate. The fact is, for both large computer systems and small ones, the cost per byte stored has fallen rather dramatically. But these cost reductions do not preclude the usefulness of networks.

A NETWORK VOCABULARY

Before networks and communications can be discussed with any degree of understanding it is necessary to define some terms. While computer jargon can often be arcane, the language of communications and computers can be downright unintelligible. Most of the terms needed to understand networks are simply extensions of ordinary English, although there are several coined terms as well as acronyms. Even if you have an understanding of networking vocabulary, this section will at least clarify how terms are being used in this book.

Computers can be said to process transactions of one form or another. Most computers through the early 1970s processed transactions in *batches*. Throughout the earlier days of computing it was common to talk about batch processing as meaning the processing of groups of punched cards. Each card was a transaction, and the computer read the batch of cards and acted upon them. During the 1960s we started to hear about *interactive* computing. With interactive computing, programs can be structured so that transactions are acted upon individually, rather than in batches. Interactive processing generally originates from data entry devices much like typewriters, called *terminals*. Unfortunately for conversation, we must sometimes refer to batch terminals as well as interactive terminals. Batch terminals, which read cards or tapes or disks and then send data to a computer in batches, are often referred to as *Remote Job Entry (RJE)* terminals or *Remote Batch Terminals (RBT)*. A general term sometimes used in reference to terminals is *remote*. We can speak of remote site, or a remote terminal, or simply a remote. A remote is any device that works remotely from the central computing facility.

Whether the processing taking place is batch or interactive, it also can take place in networks which are *centralized* or *distributed*. A centralized network is one which depends entirely on a central computing facility (of one or more computers), while a distributed network assumes that some tasks will take place on one computer while others will take place on another computer. Sometimes the two computers must talk to one another in order to receive information. Each entity on a network is called a *node*. Some nodes are computers, others are terminals, and still others may be communications devices of one form or another. When networks became important to computing during the early 1970s they were centralized. However, as the 1970s came to a close, because of declining prices of computers and because of the need for more local and regional computing in large organizations, distributed systems were discussed extensively. Even by the early 1980s, however, while there was a good bit of talk about distributed processing, it was still more of a dream than a reality for most organizations.

Within a network environment there must be some specialized communications equipment. A *modem* (an acronym for MOdulator/DEModulator) is a device that enables data to be transmitted over long distances without error. Some modems are "hard-wired" to leased telephone lines or to other cable. Others are used with dial-up telephone lines. Some are originate only — they must begin the communications process — while others have originate and answer modes (allowing another device to originate the communications link). An auto-dial modem is one that can be used in conjunction with a program (on a computer) to automatically dial another phone number which designates a line attached to another device, while an auto-answer modem can automatically answer the phone when called.

The speed at which a modem (and associated lines) can transmit data is measured in *bits per second* or *baud* rates. Sometimes it is useful or necessary to have a number of low-speed (low baud rate) channels share a single high-speed line. This is accomplished by placing a *multiplexor* between the modem and equipment such as terminals on one end of the line and/or a computer at the other end. There is often a cost savings in using a single phone line that can be shared by a number of independent channels.

Through the early 1980s most data were transmitted over telephone lines or their equivalent. About this time, however, *broad band* systems using coaxial cables were coming into use. Broad band systems use the same technology as cable television systems and can transmit data very reliably at very high speeds. Systems using fiber optics, which transmits data with high intensity light, was just becoming commercially feasible in the early 1980s but is likely to be a major technology toward the end of the decade. The advantage of fiber optics over standard telephone lines or broad band systems is that they are unaffected by most environmental elements such as water.

Data transmitted on standard telephone circuits use "voice grade" lines, which were designed primarily for voice communications. Broad band systems use very high or ultra-high radio frequencies as the communications medium. Modems are essentially devices for modulating and demodulating the electrical pulses carrying data on voice grade lines, although the literature also talks about radio frequency (RF) modems. *Base-band* systems use frequencies equal to those originally generated by the original equipment without the use of modems that manage frequency shifts.

When data are transmitted, it is done either *asynchronously* or *synchronously*. Asynchronous transmission is often referred to as *start-stop*, while the synchronous transmission characters are sent in a continuous stream. With asynchronous transmission one character is sent at a time preceded by a START signal and terminated by a STOP signal. Each time a key on an asynchronous terminal is pressed, a character is sent; another key must be pressed for a second character to be transmitted. Such machines are generally less expensive than synchronous terminals. In contrast to asynchronous machines, which usually use one character as the unit of transmission, synchronous devices use a block of characters.

When machines transmit to each other continuously, with regular timing, synchronous transmission can provide the most efficient use of the communications lines. In order to permit synchronous communications, however, devices must have buffers (some memory at least equal to one block of data) which, along with timing mechanisms, results in higher production costs. IBM has used a special form of synchronous communications called *binary synchronous*, or bisynch for short. The actual manner in which data are organized and transmitted, within the context of either asynchronous or synchronous communications, is called a *protocol*.

In order for a microcomputer to function as a terminal in a larger network it must have communications software. That software should allow the user to *upload* or *download* data. Data are uploaded when they are transmitted from the microcomputer to the central processor (or simply to another processor). They are downloaded when data are sent to the microprocessor from another source. In one sense, therefore, all uses of a terminal constitute uploading and downloading. These terms are usually used in connection with the uploading of large chunks of data — especially files which already exist on one system or the other. In fact, as will be seen in subsequent sections, the ability to upload and download significant quantities of data, or complete files of information, is an important reason for using a microcomputer as a communications device. An ability to upload and download allows data to be prepared "offline" on the micro and then uploaded to the host and vice versa.

There are other terms we will have occasion to use that will be defined as needed. Without some understanding of the various terms defined in this section, however, it would be very difficult to discuss some of the concepts related to networking.

NETWORKS IN LARGE ORGANIZATIONS

While a small organization or business may not need a network, or may need only a small local network, large organizations may need one or more of both local and global networks. Local networks are important because they can serve as the basis for expanded office automation. Systems such as Xerox's ETHERNET or Corvus Systems' OMNINET have been designed for just such purposes. As a result one can visualize a department within a larger organization (or building or some other unit) being organized into a local network sharing some resources (hard disks, printers, some software, etc.) and through this network having access to some larger global network or to other local networks. Such a system would allow efficient use of personnel, provide a means for communications among departmental personnel (or others in the larger organization), and offer considerable local computing power.

Local networks are useful in a wide variety of situations, but where the computing resources exist at long distances from the end user, then global networks (or combinations of global and local networks) may be necessary. The strength of the local area networks is that while they do not require a central, high-powered computer node, such a system may be plugged in as simply additional addresses on the system. The economy of scale argument holds in the mid 1980s about as tightly as it did in earlier periods. If the same data are needed by multiple users in a larger organization, then it will probably (although not always) be cheaper to have those data on a large system accessible across potential end users. Because the cost of computing equipment is generally declining while the cost of large-scale communications is increasing, distributed data processing (DDP) and distributed data bases (DDB) are becoming increasingly more attractive. More will be said of this later.

NETWORK ORGANIZATION

There are a variety of ways in which networks might be organized, and many (perhaps most) networks are in a constant state of change and growth. If the computer network consists of only a mainsite or host computer that does all data processing from one or more remotes, it is a centralized network. If there are remote computers processing jobs for end users as well as a main site computer (which is itself optional), then we may have the beginnings of a distributed network. A distributed network can be either centralized or hierarchical in form, but a network that does not involve distributed processing can only be centralized because all data processing is done on a main site computer. It is possible for a single communications system to provide communications for two or more concurrently operating centralized computer networks. We will review several characteristic (although oversimplified) network configurations: point-to-point, multipoint, centralized, hierarchical (distributed), interconnected (distributed), and more on local area networks.

Point-to-Point

A point-to-point network is undoubtedly the simplest kind of network, because it consists of a computer, a communications line (direct or through the telephone system), and one terminal at the other end of the wire. The terminal can be either a remote batch terminal (RBT) or interactive. This was the earliest form of network, and many networks still begin in this fashion and gradually develop into more complex entities. In such a system the central computer need not be large. A microcomputer can act as a host computer for one or more terminals. Normally, however, such systems have a reasonably substantial computer as the host system.

Multipoint Networks

Multipoint networks originally constituted a straightforward extension of point-to-point systems in that instead of a single remote station, there are multiple remote stations. Those remote stations were either RBTs or interactive or both. The remote stations may be connected via independent communications lines to the computer or may be multiplexed over a single line. In either a point-to-point or a multipoint system, the characteristics of the remote work stations are a function of the work to be accomplished at the remote site. Local networks in some of their manifestations are expansions of the multipoint concept. In its original context, a multipoint system contained only one node with "intelligence" — that is, it had only one computer on the system. A local network will normally have intelligence at all or most points on the system without the necessity for a central system at all.

Centralized (Star) Networks

To reiterate, a centralized network is one in which primary computing is accomplished at a single site with all remote stations feeding into that site. Often such a system is thought of as a star network with each remote site entering the central system via a single communications line, although point-to-point and the classical multipoint systems also are centralized networks. Typically, however, a multipoint network does not have distributed processing capabilities, while a star network may have other computers out at the end of its communications lines. In fact, the computer that supports a traditional multipoint network might, itself, be linked into a star network.

Hierarchical (Distributed) Networks

A hierarchical network represents a fully distributed network in which computers feed into computers which in turn feed into computers. The computers used for remote devices may have independent processing capabilities and draw upon the resources at higher or lower levels as information or other resources are required. A hierarchical network is one form of completely distributed network. The classical model of a hierarchical distributed network is that used by Texas Instruments in which there are several IBM 3033s and 3081s at the top and IBM 4341s or similar machines in the mid-range, fed by a combination of minis (such as the TI990), micros, and other machines at the bottom. The TI990s actually may function as a third level and the micros (or intelligent terminals) as a fourth level.

Interconnected (Distributed) Networks

There are several forms of "interconnected" networks, but the distinguishing feature is that such networks possess more than one intelligent node. Consequently, at least as far as hardware is concerned, they are (or should be) distributed systems. A completely connected network is one in which each node is tied directly back to every other node. A circular network interconnects each node through others in a closed chain. A multipoint interconnected network ties each node to a common line providing direct communications between each node.

One of the principal advantages of any of the interconnected models is reliability. Because the network is not dependent on any one element of the system, it will continue to function even when one (or more) of its components is not functioning properly. The same would be true of a hierarchical system, at least up to a point. If the system (or systems) at the top went out, however, those tasks dependent on the centralized facilities would be down even though components continued to function independently.

Local Area Networks (Distributed)

As we have already noted, local area networks are distinguished, in part, by the fact that they do not require a central computer node. In that sense they can be thought of as a special case of an interconnected network. During the 1980s however, local area networks will become an important and integral part of a wide range of information processing systems. They will play a major role particularly in the area of office automation. But local area networks are not limited to systems like ETHERNET or LOCALNET/20. They can be very expansive and form the basic networking approach for a multibuilding, campus-like institution, whether in the public or private sector. The technology that in the early 1980s offered the most generalized approach to local area networking was broad band cable television (CATV). Manufacturers such as Sytek, Inc., with their LocalNet 20 and LocalNet 40 provided systems for user-to-computer, user-to-user, or (very high-speed) computer-to-computer communications. Moreover, such systems can be linked, through appropriate gateways, to a community-wide CATV system.

A typical cable television system has sufficient frequency bandwidth to handle 35 to 54 television channels. Thus, in terms of data throughput, the frequency band that one TV channel occupies can be used to provide the equivalent capacity of an entire baseband network or more. An unused TV channel could also be divided into 20 data subchannels and each subchannel into about 200 user data links. This translates into a capacity of about 4000 user-to-computer links at 9.6K baud. There must be one

TV channel for sending and one for return. Broad band systems support both asynchronous and synchronous communications.

Basically a simple broad band system would use two television channels, each with a 6 MHz (megahertz or 1 million hertz) bandwidth. One channel supports forward communications, the other return communications. Each channel is subdivided into twenty 300 KHz (kilohertz or 1000 hertz) data channels. Frequency Division Multiplexing (FDM) is used to subdivide each of the twenty channels into about 200 datalinks.

There are two standard bandwidths used to support CATV systems. One spectrum runs from 5 to 300 MHz supporting 39 television channels. The other runs from 5 to 400 MHz supporting 54 television channels. Use of the spectrum is mapped in one of two ways: subsplit or midsplit. Commercial CATV systems use a subsplit system that provides two-way communications in the inbound direction from 5 to 30 MHz and outbound transmission from 54 to 300 (or 400) MHz. The midsplit system uses 5 to 108 MHz for inbound and 162 to 400 MHz for outbound. The advantages of midsplit mapping is that there are more inbound channels than with subsplit. A subsplit and midsplit system can be interfaced with a gateway device so that nodes on one can communicate with nodes on the other.

DISTRIBUTED DATA PROCESSING (DDP)

At several points we have spoken of centralized and distributed processing as if the two concepts in networks were at opposite ends of some continuum, although this is not the case. Nor can distributed processing be thought of simply as decentralized computing. One definition, as suggested by Data 100 as reported by John M. Lusa, *et al.* ("Distributed Processing: Alive and Well." *Infosystems* 23, November 1976, 35–41) states that distributed computing places "a substantial part of the pre- and post-processing of data, and access to data at the places where the data originates and is used . . . while maintaining central control of the networks."

It is not uncommon for networks which start as relatively simple centralized systems to migrate to distributed systems without conscious design on the part of systems analysts. As often as not, a typical batch terminal in a network may be replaced with a mini- or microprocessor-based device providing local file storage and processing capabilities as well as the capacity to generate batch jobs (or interactive jobs, for that matter).

The decision to acquire a terminal with intelligence may be, in fact, the decision of the end user rather than that of the network analysts. If there is the possibility of communicating with the central system with some intelligent device (such as a microcomputer), an end user may make the decision to do distributed data processing. Thus the decision to turn a centralized network into a distributed processing network may be even further removed from decisions made by analysts at the central site. The key point is that if a network migrates into a distributed system, it is unlikely that there will be the element of central control desirable for many functions, particularly access to central databases (or to distributed databases).

Both local and global networks may be distributed networks, but they perform somewhat different functions for an organization. We have already noted that as the cost of computing hardware has been declining, the cost for communications has been on the rise. This has led some industry analysts to "sense that the traditional concept of linking many company locations into a common network to utilize centralized facilities was waning in its desirability" (Dale G. Mullen, "Is Your Telecommunications Network Obsolete?", *Telematics*, Vol. 1, No. 4, September 1981, pp. 17–19). Yet it is also clear that the "'gurus of the future' are correct when they forecast a pivotal role for networking in future information distribution solutions" (Mullen, p. 18). The networks of the 1980s and 1990s will tend to be decentralized because data processing and data bases will become increasingly distributed. The organizational implications of such a situation are manifold, but one major implication is the decentralization of responsibility (within the organization) for the maintenance and function of the networks. On a global scale, networks will be implicit rather than explicit and communication will take place when needed rather than being hard-wired (with leased telephone lines, for example).

On the other hand, local networks will themselves distribute processing among a number of intelligent nodes, probably (though not necessarily) hard-wired together. Such a local network can then become an intelligent node of a global network. The local network, composed primarily of microcomputers (whether called word processors, data processors, or just plain micros), is capable of participating in what Paul Truax of Truax & Associates Inc., calls the "four corporate information disciplines." These four disciplines are office automation, data processing, data base administration, and telecommunications. (From an address to the 1980 DPMA international conference, as quoted by Wayne L. Rhodes, Jr., "Office of the Future: Light Years Away?" *Infosystems*, Vol. 28, No. 3, March 1981, pp. 40–50.)

Microcomputers in Global Networks

Microcomputers play many roles in large-scale global networks and will have expanded roles into the 1990s. The primary use will likely become (if this is not already the case) that of a general purpose store and forward processor. That is, many functions (especially text editing) traditionally handled by central time-sharing systems can be handled locally by microcomputers. Rather than consuming both computer time and communications time by preparing data and text on a central system, consistent with the ideas mentioned above concerning the development of implicit (or virtual) networks, data and text can be prepared locally on a micro then forwarded to a central system for processing. Such use is appropriate for a wide variety of transactions including job setup, electronic mail, and other applications that require a text to be created and edited before any data processing is accomplished.

The forwarding function could be accomplished in a virtually automatic fashion with relatively simple software by having an auto-dial modem connected to the microcomputer. When a local function is completed, a generalized forward command could invoke a communications program which would dial a remote computer, log on to the system, transmit the data, wait for some specified response, log off, and hangup the telephone. Electronic mail sent in this manner could be sent economically over standard telephone service even at baud rates as low as 300 bps (bits per second).

Another function within a global (or local) network that already has considerable importance is as a control device for the communications system itself. Several manufacturers of port selectors (devices for the management of computer ports on a large network) require that the network administrator have a terminal to control some functions of the network. Very frequently that terminal is a microcomputer that uploads port addresses to the system and logs system problems. This kind of use, while less obvious than applications in office automation, is no less important.

Microcomputers in Local Networks

Although microcomputers are important in global networks, they are central in local networks; which are often focused on micros. Whether we talk about ETHERNET, OMNINET, Burroughs' OFIS, or a host of other local networks being marketed or developed, we are talking about microcomputers. In such systems the clear trend is away from a centralized minicomputer to a number of approximately (although this is not necessary) equal nodes. In some systems, especially those marketed by large vendors such as Xerox, advertising emphasis seems to be upon microprocessors dedicated to specific functions, such as word processing, although the word processors have communications functions.

By the end of 1981, however, it was clear that even the large vendors were moving away from processors dedicated to specific functions and moving toward general purpose microcomputers capable of doing a number of different functions. Late in 1981, for example, IBM not only announced its first "personal computer" (which has asynchronous communications facilities as a standard and is provided with bisynchronous communications as an option), but also announced its business System 23 (which came with both a synchronous and bisynchronous communications as standard items). Although the System 23 was initially marketed with the "small business" as a target, it was clear that the machine was equipped to work within both local and global networks. In early 1982 Tandy announced its TRS-80 Model 16, which also is equipped for both asynchronous and bisynchronous communications.

AN OVERVIEW OF NETWORK APPLICATIONS

Although Chapter 3 will discuss several of the applications noted here in further detail and others not necessarily related to networks, it is important to comment in this chapter on several applications specifically relevant to the networking environment. Any detailed evaluations of these applications will be left for Chapter 3; here we will provide something of the flavor of applications of particular value within a distributed network. Some of these applications have already been mentioned as illustrating why microcomputers might be of significance. Other applications will be introduced at this point.

Electronic Mail
and Computer Conferencing

Although electronic mail was being extensively discussed in the late 1970s and early 1980s, it was given more lip service than use. A principal factor that prohibits extensive use of electronic mail is not technological but human. Many people have a difficult time learning to use a terminal or microcomputer regularly, and electronic mail systems require regular use. It is especially difficult, of course, when not everyone in an organization is equipped with appropriate terminals. With the marketing of local networks, the wider dispersal of terminals within a network (whether dumb terminals or microcomputers), and the increasing burden and cost of intraorganizational paper communications, sending messages through a computer system will become more commonplace. As noted earlier, micros can be especially useful electronic mail nodes, simply because they do not have to be connected into a network on a permanent or semipermanent basis (as do dumb terminals) to be used. When an "intelligent" machine is used as a node in an electronic mail system, then messages can be prepared locally, shipped automatically, and received automatically.

There have been several suggestions as to how such a system might work, and the comments presented here are not original. Imagine, for example, that a microcomputer was equipped with a simple text editor and an intelligent communications program. The micro also would need an inexpensive auto-answer, auto-dial modem (which operates at 300 baud and costs less than $300). A modem is a device which interfaces a terminal to a telephone (or similar) line, modulating and demodulating the binary language of the computer. Once the text of a message is prepared using the text editor, the micro might be given an instruction to transmit the message at some predetermined time (to take full advantage of lower communications rates), dial a target microcomputer, send the message, and terminate the call. Although there were no off-the-shelf electronic mail packages available at the close of 1981, this software was under development. Such software, along with a micro, could be used in a fashion analogous to standard telephone communications but with the added advantage of producing a document.

A more standard approach to electronic mail was fairly widely available on computer networks by the early 1980s. In such systems some software is provided, which allows one user to create a message, address it to another user, and have some verification that the message is received (and presumably read). On a national scale Western Union's Mailgram service was expanded to allow direct electronic access, which provided for next-day delivery of a printed version of the message. In some large organizations electronic mail and message systems are the standard method of intraorganizational communications, but such use requires considerable organizational commitment.

An important expansion of the concept of electronic mail is computer conferencing. A computer conferencing system not only provides the basic message service, but also a means for having online discussions, recording proceedings, voting on issues in a variety of ways, and other similar services. Even simple mail systems can be used in applications where collective action is required (such as some types of organizational planning and forecasting), but conferencing systems make such activities more systematic and provide the kinds of summary data often required. Unfortunately, by the early 1980s there were only a very few, expensive, conferencing systems available on the open market, although several institutions and individuals had operative systems. When used in a network environment, mail and conferencing systems are highly dependent on the central operating system and therefore are not very transportable. In a local network both a message and a conferencing system could be created with one microcomputer on the local network acting as the conference/message controller accessible to all other nodes.

Office Automation

Although the vendors of office automation systems had not convinced everyone of the appropriateness of their products by the early 1980s, offices were becoming partially automated through the back door by people acquiring microcomputers for a variety of uses. The "office-of-the-future" may actually be closer than most of us believe, if by that phrase we mean the increased use of computer technology for solving office bottlenecks.

However, if we mean the use of integrated systems, then the "office-of-the-future" may be further off. In fact, as was implied previously, the backbone of office automation will be the local network. And within that local network the nodes will be microcomputers of one form or another. The network concepts that are likely to outlast the 1980s, however, are those which allow access to the network by devices of many different manufacturers doing a number of different chores. The reason for this is that so many micros are being acquired by large organizations (independently of coherent schemes of office automation), that a demand will arise for the networks to support a variety of devices. Ultimately, however, a wide variety of office machines, including intelligent terminals (micros), will acquire sufficient capability to function in a network. This includes copying machines, communications devices, and a variety of equipment just making its appearance on the drawing boards.

Perhaps the primary place of microcomputers in office automation in the early 1980s is their role as word processors. Many such micros were being sold as stand-alone word processors with no other function. The advantages of word processors over standard typewriters or other machines for composing, editing, and producing text material are myriad. If a writer already composes at a typewriter, a micro equipped with a decent printer can preclude the use of a typist for some functions. In particular, once text is typed into a word processing system, it is easy to modify, change, expand, or contract the document. Thus, at least in principle, reproducible text is possible. Added to this advantage is the development of programs with significantly large vocabularies to check spelling. Thus any standard, off-the-shelf micro can be an important assistant to anyone who does a significant amount of writing.

Microcomputers
and the Programming Staff

By the early 1980s several computer manufacturers were offering microcomputers to be used primarily in tandem with other larger computers. The objective here was to provide programmers with a software development tool in recognition of the increased costs of both communications and personnel. With such a micro a programmer can develop programs for the larger system and do initial compiles (including considerable debugging), without having to use either the resources of the larger system or a great deal of communications time. Prior to about 1980 such a system would have imposed considerable constraints since most micros did not allow memory sizes larger than 64K (K equals 1024) eight bit bytes (with each byte the equivolent of one typed character). Thus, the development of very large programs was difficult and would have had to be subdivided into quite small chunks. By 1981, however, there were a number of micros on the market that went considerably beyond 64K (to 128K, 256K, or even 1024K). The consequence of these developments was that significantly large programs could be initially developed (though perhaps not run) on micros prior to final testing on the target computer. At the very least, however, some organizations were encouraging programmers to use micros along with online program development to maintain running documentation of the programs being written or maintained.

This chapter has provided an overview of some uses of microcomputers in networks and within a distributed data processing environment. Included has been a glimpse of some of the applications for which we might use micros. The list presented here is not exhaustive. In fact this entire book cannot contain anything approaching a complete catalogue of microcomputer applications. Chapter 3, however, continues the discussion of micro applications within a large organization including not only more detailed treatments of applications in networks, but also a number of uses for micros as stand-alone systems. That chapter provides hypothetical scenarios of microcomputer use, and Chapter 6 looks at some ways in which micros are actually being used by large organizations.

In closing this chapter we can conclude that micros will have an ever-expanding role to play within global networks and local networks, but both will operate within the context of distributed data processing.

3

Uses of Microcomputers

A microcomputer is a *personal tool,* and within large organizations it remains one, much like a typewriter or a calculator. Computing in general has passed through at least three stages of growth: dedicated processor, service bureau, and utility. In the earliest stage, when a user and a computer met, the computer was monopolized by a single user for some period of time, although several users could process jobs in a sequence. As computers grew larger, acquired more functions, and became somewhat more obscure and arcane to individuals, computing organizations took on a service bureau approach, doing much (if not all) the work for a user. This was the model of the 1960s and 1970s.

With the advent of very large machines, more user-friendly operating systems, and time sharing, computing was reorganized (beginning in the mid-1970s) with computer facilities becoming utilities that provided a resource much like an electric utility provides electricity. With the appearance of microcomputers, a complete circle has occurred, returning to the stage of the dedicated processor. This time, however, the dedicated machine is sufficiently inexpensive so that it need never be shared with others. At the same time it exists within a larger computing environment, which also allows access to computer utilities regardless of whether they are true public utilities (such as networks like The Source or Compuserve) or private utilities (such as those within large corporations or universities). It is within this more expansive computing environment that micros can function effectively to enhance increasingly complex work loads.

USING MICROCOMPUTERS–
ONCE OVER LIGHTLY

In 1978 Robert C. Gammill (in a paper entitled "Personal Computers for Science in the 1980's") suggested that rapid "advances in LSI electronics technology promise the availability of marginally suitable hardware configurations at an appropriate price ($1000 to $4000) in the next twelve years." Gammill's reference was to the possible availability of microcomputers to be used by scientists working within larger organizations. Gammill suggested that there were three requirements for personal computers to be useful to such people. First, they had to be dependable tools for generating, manipulating, and examining text and limited data collections. Second, such computers would have to serve as terminals in a network environment. Third, microcomputers would have to serve as dependable and unsleeping agents for data and message collection. His judgment was that (in 1978) personal computers did not yet meet the three requirements.

By the early 1980s the situation had changed markedly, however. And the people using microcomputers were not only scientists, but a wide variety of professionals engaged in diversified tasks. The key element, however, is that while it took only two to four years (rather than twelve) for the technology to provide Gammill's requirements, the potential uses far exceeded what many people perceived even in the late 1970s. As might be expected, the list of applications was incomplete for micros available at the writing of this book. Inventories can be compiled partly by scanning the pages of the extensive number of magazines being published that deal with microcomputing. Partial catalogs also can be obtained by simply asking users of micros how they are being used.

In an effort to itemize software for this book, I surveyed members of the Dallas Chapter of the Data Processing Management Association. Using only responses from employees of large organizations, I was able to compile a partial software tally. Data processing managers may not know how many microcomputers there are in a large organization, much less the variety of uses to which they are being put. On the other hand, the list I was able to compile is fairly impressive and provides a good overview of the situation.

Text and Data Management

This area, of course, involves the most important and comprehensive use to which microcomputers may be put, because it encompasses almost everything except data collection and communications. In my sampling of Dallas enterprises this was clearly the area for which most people acquired micros, with the single most frequent reference being to applications in financial analysis (planning and modeling). Closely allied uses include operations research, production planning, simulations, and statistics. All in all, out of 103 uses mentioned, there were 13 specific references to financial modeling and planning with an additional 7 references to related uses. A close second in the number of mentions (11) was word processing.

Other uses identified included limited data base management (such as inquiry), accounting, biomedical preventive maintenance, budgeting, dealer support, drilling reports (oil exploration), education (training devices in both universities and industry), engineering analysis, insurance evaluations, inventory control, organizational maintenance, personnel, project control, sales and marketing, staff scheduling, software development, stock analysis, and tax computations. There were several specific references to various database applications; these are not listed separately.

The most telling point made by one respondent was that her firm used microcomputers as managers' work stations. She went on to list the specific functions as electronic filing, project control, and word processing. In fact, for all the items listed above, the general term "manager's work station" would serve as an umbrella for almost all of the applications listed. During the mid-1980s the concept of a manager's work station is likely to take hold in a number of organizations in a major way as middle management seeks better tools for coping with increased demands in a sometimes shrinking economy. As personnel costs increase, there will be greater need to use clerical and secretarial help more efficiently. This will lead, in turn, to greater use of the management work station concept.

With the advent of relatively low-cost, general-purpose microcomputers with considerable capacity, many of the more trivial clerical chores will be taken over by micros. On a somewhat higher level, computing problems in forecasting, project control, and related areas of concern either will move from being done with the assistance of a calculator to the more sophisticated help provided by a micro or will move from central mainframe computers to the more economical (and private) personal computers. In a large organization, therefore, the entire area of text and data management as accomplished on micros can be viewed functionally as the application of the manager's work station concept.

Microcomputers and Communications

We already have assessed (in Chapter 2) the role microcomputers can play in larger networks. As late as 1978 Gammill was able to report that there were few (if any) adequate communications packages running on micros. In the 1979 to 1981 time period, however, a number of sophisticated communications packages hit the software market for a variety of micros. As a by-product of this availability there were five specific references (in the Dallas survey) to the use of micros as intelligent terminals and one respondent specifically identified "distributed processing" as a goal of microcomputer acquisitions. We earlier mentioned IBM 3270 support as announced for both Radio Shack (TRS-80 model II and 16) computers and IBM personal computers during mid-1981 which expanded the sophistication of communications support available for microcomputers. The IBM 3270 terminal uses synchronous communications and is designed specifically to work on large IBM mainframe computers.

All of the problems concerning the use of micros as intelligent terminals were not solved by the early 1980s, however. The various 8-bit processors used as the base for most of the microcomputers during the period simply were not fast enough to provide reliable data communications at rates faster than about 1200 baud (bits per second), with the standard at 300 baud. The microcomputer central processing units (CPUs) available at the beginning of 1982 used word lengths of 8 bits, 16 bits, or 32 bits. The most commonly used processors, such as the Z80 or 6802 were 8-bit processors. While these slower communications rates are appropriate for many applications, they are still much too slow for transferring an appreciable amount of data in short periods of time (an important issue in a communications system). By the end of 1981 the much heralded 16-bit processors were beginning to have a sufficiently good price/performance ratio to compete effectively in the microcomputer market. It will likely be sometime in the late 1980s that the newer 32-bit processors drop in price sufficiently to make them competitive. Nevertheless, these problems aside, microcomputers can still be effective intelligent terminals within a large network.

Data Collection and Control

The term "data collection" has several meanings—from using a micro-computer as a data entry device keyed by an operator to having it attached as a real-time control device in a laboratory or on a production line. In trying to illustrate such uses of microcomputers, this book has tied the control function to data collection simply because in many control situations data also are collected concurrently with the control function. The use of microcomputers for data collection and control appears to be a major part of the use of the machines in large organizations. Of the 103 uses of micros in the Dallas sample, 18 were for data collection and/or control systems. Two simply listed "data collection," two more listed "intelligent data entry," and two (one in an industrial laboratory and one in a university laboratory) listed use as a laboratory control device. Other uses included control devices for other computer systems, for communications systems, and for security systems, all with data collection as a by-product. Someone used a micro on a shop floor to gather work information, while another used a micro to gather performance information on a large computer. One large retailer used micros for point-of-sale activities. Another used micros to validate data before batch job submission to a large system.

In the early 1980s perhaps the most serious problems with using a microcomputer as a data collection device, especially in an unattended mode, were limitations on the amount of long-term storage typically available at a low cost. By the early eighties the standard storage device had become either the 5.25-inch or the 8-inch floppy disk. So-called "Winchester" drives, using a hard, sealed disk, were able to store 5 to 20 megabytes of data as compared with a quarter million bytes or less data on the typical floppy disk (depending on size and formatting). The price of the Winchester disks, however, was still in the $2000 to $6000 range. Using Winchester drives certainly reduced the cost per byte of external storage on large mainframes. But the prices on the Winchesters also were continuing to decline during the period, making their price/performance ratios very attractive. The relatively slow speed of the floppies also preclude them from some data collection applications, although it frequently is possible to get around such limitations with appropriate software.

Problems and Opportunities

By the early 1980s there were software products on the microcomputer market that would assist in all areas previously described. Not only were many software products available, but they were priced far below comparable software on large mainframes. An example of price differentials were electronic spreadsheet programs (mentioned in Chapter 1) which sold for large IBM mainframes at prices ranging from $14,000 to $40,000. For microcomputers, almost equivalent programs sold for $100 to $300. The large mainframe versions could have a total market of only a few thousand (and more realistically a few hundred) sales before the market was saturated, while the potential market for the micro software was in the hundreds of thousands.

Problems arose, however, when the objective was to provide an integrated manager's work station or some similar application. One useful item might run on one operating system and another item on a different operating system. Even if everything was available on a given operating system it was sometimes necessary to provide two or more word processing packages to do everything that might be needed, thus creating a learning problem for the potential user. An integrated package also requires that the components be linked together in an easily accessible form (perhaps menu driven), thus requiring some programming assistance and some systems assistance.

A "menu" driven system is one which provides a set of multiple choice alternatives—the user chooses one by pressing one key or another (or perhaps typing a word). An example is the package I regularly use on the micro in my office. It contains a word processor (NEWSCRIPT from Prosoft), an electronic spreadsheet program (VISICALC from Personal Software), a data manager (PROFILE from Radio Shack), a sophisticated communications program (ST80III from Lance Micklus, Inc.), an appointments calendar program, a notebook (scratch pad) program, and a printer initialization program to let me change type fonts on my printer. All these programs are tied together with a menu program (which I wrote) and are installed on an operating system disk which provides for automatic execution of the menu program when the system is started. While none of this is very complicated, it could not be accomplished by a novice, who is precisely the person needing a friendly, integrated approach. Some of these issues will be addressed in more detail in subsequent sections of this chapter as we go into more detail on potential applications for micros in large organizations.

MICROCOMPUTER APPLICATIONS AND FUNCTIONS

Previously it was suggested that there are three broad application areas with which we must be concerned when depicting the role of microcomputers in large organizations: text and data mangement, communications, and data collection and control. This section describes more explicitly the functions that must be performed if those three broad areas are to be properly addressed. We will take each of the three areas in turn and attempt to describe and illustrate specific functions with reference to specific products. Bear in mind that each program runs under a particular operating system such as TRSDOS on Radio Shack TRS-80 microcomputers or CP/M on a large number of other computers. The operating system organizes the computer for the user and allows communications with applications programs. Consequently, ordinarily it would not be a good idea to establish an environment requiring multiple operating systems, although this may be necessary under some conditions.

Text and Data Management

WORD PROCESSING. The primary text management system is an appropriate word processor. Several manufacturers during the late 1970s and early 1980s produced stand-alone word processing machines which were essentially microcomputers dedicated to a single task. The difficulty with the dedicated processor philosophy is that there are a number of functions needed in any office, and especially by management, which require a general-purpose computer rather than a dedicated machine. The issue then becomes one of deciding whether good word processing software exists that can be run on a microcomputer or whether, in a given situation, both a general-purpose microprocessor and a dedicated word processor are necessary. I suspect that in most situations the best decision would be to acquire the general-purpose micro. Interestingly, the general-purpose micro is typically less expensive than the dedicated word processor.

Any word processing package consists of two modules: one for editing text (an electronic typewriter) and one for formatting it. These two modules may be designed as independent programs or may be two elements in one large program. To the novice the combined word processing package is probably less confusing initially, although the separate program approach in many cases may provide either more elaborate editing or formatting functions or both. Whether the approach is a consolidated program or an independent program, the word processing package should include some standard functions and beyond that can include extensive capabilties specific to a particular system. How elaborate or how simple a system to choose is in part a by-product of its intended use. If the primary objective is to produce short documents such as letters or memoranda, then a simple, straightforward system which provides a close analog to a typewriter might be the best choice. However, if the objective is to prepare extensive manuals, books, or other lengthy documents, then a more elaborate system is probably required. If at all possible, it would be best to standardize on one (or possibly two) word processing packages across a large organization in order to reduce learning time as people move horizontally in the organization.

The Text Editor.   Central to any word processing system and to a great deal of other work accomplished with a micro is good text editor. A text editor allows the input of text from a keyboard and, once entered, allows for the correction, deletion, addition or, in general, the manipulation of the text. The text can be words and paragraphs (like this book) or can be a file of instructions for the computer or can even be numeric data to be analyzed at a later date. The text editor can become a general-purpose input program and should be selected with that concept in mind. There are two basic kinds of text editors: line oriented and full screen. The older form of text editor was the line editor. The operator could only work on one line at a time and had access to only one line at a time. As might be anticipated, editing a long document with a line editor can be tedious. A full-screen editor, on the other hand, presents a full video screen of data or text to the operator. By using selected keys (often marked with arrows: up, down, left, and right), the operator can move the cursor (a marker showing where on the screen the next entry will be) to desired location. What is seen on the screen is often a fairly precise rendition of the final document.

A properly conceived text editor will have easily used facilities for adding, deleting, changing, moving, or replacing text, always at the level of individual characters and sometimes for entire words, sentences (or lines), and paragraphs. In addition to being able to perform such functions by moving the cursor around the screen, the text editor also should have the facility to do "global" changes and deletions. That is, it should be possible to issue one command to change all occurrences of "KWIT" for example, to "QUIT," regardless of how many times "KWIT" occurs in the text. If the total word processing system requires that the edited file be in some special format, then the editor also should be capable of producing a standard ASCII file readable by other programs written in whatever languages are supported by the computer system. Remember, this is likely to be one of the most frequently used programs in any library and, therefore, should be highly flexible. There are other attributes that might be useful for a text editor to have, but these are the minimum requirements for a useful program.

Editors can be either command driven or menu driven. In a command driven system one line of the display is usually provided as an area where the user can enter whatever editing commands are needed. With such a system the user must either remember all the commands (something which comes with frequent use) and/or use a reference card or manual. In a menu-driven system part of the screen is reserved for one or more menus, which allow the user to issue editing commands by making a selection from the menu. Usually the menu can be suppressed, but then the user must remember the menu or bring it back to the screen periodically. The editor used to prepare the text for this book, for example, was a command-driven editor.

The Text Formatter.   The text formatter, when run against an edited file, will take formatting instructions embedded in the text and produce a final printed copy according to the formatting requirements. We do the same thing when we use a typewriter according to formatting rules learned at some time. College composition classes often stress the use of a style manual which is designed to teach (among other things) text formatting. Some text formatters can automatically format text according to some specific style manual or to a specific style imposed by the user.

It is the formatter which makes the printed document attractive and readable. In integrated word processing systems the formatting commands entered into the text file are often invisible to the operator and are generated by menu selection or by special function keys on the keyboard when the document was being edited. Some integrated systems also may require the entry of explicit formatting commands in the text. The system used for this book, for example, uses the command ".pp" to specify the beginning of a paragraph. All formatters that are independent of a text editor require explicit formatting commands. Invisible implicit commands sometimes can make the entire system more transparent to a novice user, although an extensive library of explicit formatting commands usually means having the capability to format more complex documents. Any formatter must provide margin control (top, bottom, left, and right); carriage control of the printer; formatting control including entry of blank lines, centering text, justification, spacing, and possibly automatic hyphenation; special features such as index preparation, table of contents, macro execution (sets of formatting commands), file access for acquiring text from other than the main file, and the ability to chain files so that one long document can be produced from several short ones. Beyond these abilities, many formatters have other features to enhance document preparation.

Examples of word processing systems currently available for microcomputers include Radio Shack's SCRIPSIT for Models I, II, and III. All versions are integrated systems encompassing both text editors and formatters. The formatters work with both implicit and explicit commands. Earlier versions of the Model I/III SCRIPSIT used editing commands while the Model II version was menu driven. The system did not have the ability to chain files or to include external files as a text was being formatted. As noted earlier, this book was written on TRS-80 Model III using a word processing system called NEWSCRIPT (by Prosoft). NEWSCRIPT is explicitly patterned after full-screen editors found on large IBM mainframes, and the formatter is patterned after SCRIPT (both the IBM and University of Waterloo versions). The editor and the formatter are independent of one another, although each will call the other and pass file names.

The editing capabilities of NEWSCRIPT are more extensive than those of SCRIPSIT, as are the formatting capabilities. Both systems, of course, run under the TRSDOS operating system. A typical (and highly acclaimed) word processing package for CP/M systems is WORDSTAR (by MicroPro International Corporation). WORDSTAR, like SCRIPSIT, is an integrated editor/formatter. The editor is menu driven, and many formatting commands are implicit (hidden), although there is a set of explicit formatting commands (dot commands). Both NEWSCRIPT and WORDSTAR provide for extensive printer control including generating subscripts and superscripts when supported by the hardware. There are a number of other word processing systems on the market, although those mentioned are good examples. All those mentioned above have full screen editing.

DATA MANAGEMENT AND ANALYSIS. It would be easy to write an entire book on the data management and analysis possibilities of microcomputers. One of the primary uses of any computer is, after all, data management. While the term "data management" has many meanings, we will look at three broad areas: planning and modeling software, data base software, and statistical and related analytical software. There are a number of other possibilities, but the three areas mentioned are probably those most needed in management functions.

Planning and Modeling Software. There are a variety of possibilities when discussing planning and modeling software. Forecasting software is available to do economic and other forecasting, although the most sophisticated models will still require original programming. Related to forecasting models is the general area of operations research used widely in corporate and other large-scale planning efforts. Many (probably most) operations research techniques, such as linear programming, can be implemented in one fashion or another on microcomputers, although there are few off-the-shelf packages available. There also was some question about adequacy of such software in the early 1980s. Software availability in these areas is largely a matter of time and market conditions. It is likely some institutions currently using micros produce their own software packages. The most interesting and widespread software packages, used especially in financial planning, are the electronic spreadsheet programs including VISICALC (by Personal Software) and SUPERCALC (by Sorcim Corporation).

The electronic spreadsheet programs provide the user with the ability to enter and manipulate a large matrix of numbers and labels, and then do a variety of calculation on the numeric data. Formulas can be set up and saved to do a variety of mathematics by row or column of the spreadsheet. In financial planning this is especially useful since some of the data entered will be estimates of such future conditions such as sales, or revenue. In order to produce a best estimate of the near future it is often necessary to estimate worst-case, best-case, and middle-case scenarios. Thus it is possible to address the "what if" aspect of forecasting in a simple and straightforward manner. In fact, the term "electronic spreadsheet" comes from the perspective that such programs can emulate anything a human can do on a paper spreadsheet with pencil and paper.

Much of what we do in planning and analysis constitutes the manipulation of tabular data, and the spreadsheet programs allow such manipulation to be accomplished in a relatively easy manner. VISICALC has been produced for many popular microcomputers such as the APPLE and the TRS-80, while SUPERCALC functions under CP/M. One of the major problems with current software operating on micros is the limited matrix size imposed by memory limitations. These limitations could be reduced by dynamically storing parts of the matrix on disk to create large virtual matrixes. It is likely that sooner or later VISICALC and SUPERCALC and similar prgrams will be altered to use swapping between disk and memory so that larger models can be constructed.

Data Management and Retrieval.   In the early 1980s there were a number of "data base management" systems on the market designed for various microcomputers. Several of them had many virtues; all had many limitations. The limitations were in part a function of the microcomputer, but more frequently they were a function of the design concepts employed in generating the data base. A data base management system is a program which creates, modifies, sorts, and retrieves data. The typical data base manager allows the user to create a "screen" which permits easy data entry, display, and updating capabilities. The files produced may be organized in a variety of ways, but the design is generally structured to provide fast access and (from the user's perspective) access with English-like labels (sometimes called keys). Some data base managers provide computational facilities; others do not.

It is essential for the buyer to beware when searching for a data base manager for a microcomputer. If the objective is simply to be able to store, retrieve, and report (on a screen or printer) a limited number of data items, then most of the systems commonly advertised will suffice. However, if the objective is to build files that will be accessed by other application programs, then the problems multiply. The first requirement for the data base system is that the structure of the output file and layout of resulting records be well documented so that other programs can access the data. The second requirement is that the data base manager be able to generate a sufficient number of data items per *logical* record to be of use in a given application. If we are using a data base manager to create name and address files, with some limited demographic data on each person, then almost any of the data base managers on the market will suffice. If we are attempting to build a numeric data base that may have 100 or 200 or more data elements per logical record, then the data base managers that were on the market in the early 1980s were not sufficient.

The typical microcomputer data base manager in the early 1980s allowed both physical and logical records of not more than 256 bytes per record. A physical record length is hardware-dependent, but many physical records can be linked together to form a very long logical record —this is a function of software, not hardware. A more important limitation, however, was the fact that a maximum of 20 to 32 data elements (whether they filled the 256 bytes or not) were allowed for each record. Each data element constitutes one item of data. For example, if we were creating a name and address file, LAST NAME might be one data element (or field), FIRST NAME another, STREET ADDRESS another, and so on. On the other hand, suppose we were creating a numeric data file consisting of data collected from each employee concerning level of satisfaction with working conditions. A typical questionnaire might have 115 or 120 items. There's plenty of room on the record, but no way to define 120 fields. Consequently, a piece of data base software which is good in principle fails in practice as a *general* method for organizing, maintaining, and structuring data.

A closely related issue is the versatility and documentation for whatever records are produced by the data base manager. One of Radio Shack's early entries into the market was a program called MICROFILES. It stored and retrieved data, but its file structure was not accessible by any other software. This issue goes both ways. Complete data base systems on large mainframe computers, such as Software AG's ADABASE or IBM's IMS provide an entire environment in which applications may be developed. While such systems provide the ability to store, organize, and retrieve data, applications that do something with the data must frequently be written. With data entry, however, the display of the data and certainly the organization of the data are sometimes handled by the data base systems. In the early 1980s there was no comparable software for microcomputers. When microcomputers were used in the context of large organizations, it must be remembered that data handling systems were still somewhat limited in scope and character. By late 1981, however, products were being advertised (such as MDBS III by Micro Data Base Systems, Inc.) that promised to remedy some of the criticisms noted above.

Statistical and Numerical Analysis.   In the early 1980s the most primitive applications packages on the market were statistical software. There were very few systems available which even claimed to be integrated statistical packages. Examples of such claims were MICROSTAT (by ECOSOFT) STATPRO (by Blue Lakes Computer), and THE STATISTICIAN (by Quant Systems). One supplier was offering a scientific subroutine package which was, apparently, a BASIC translation of the old IBM Scientific Subroutine Package (SSP). In addition, BYTE Magazine published a two-volume set of scientific subroutines. Early on, shortly after the introduction of the Model I, Radio Shack also published a statistical package. Most packages were not well integrated, some contained computational errors, and some lacked the ability to do transformations and recoding which are frequently needed facilities.

In addition to the straight statistical systems there were a variety of stand-alone programs that provided one type of statistical analysis or another, or offered operations research models such as linear programming, critical path analysis, Gantt charts, and similar facilities. Some of these programs also were being published in the various microcomputer magazines, although either highly simplified or very truncated and certainly not integrated packages. Moreover, none provided methods to access data created by data base programs or by programs such as VISICALC or, conversely, generated data in a form that could be accessed by these other programs. One of the programs is the nature of the market: the larger software publishers have not perceived the demand for a sophisticated statistical package. Models do exist, of course. There are several statistical packages available on large mainframe computers such as SPSS (Statistical Package for the Social Sciences), SAS (Statistical Analysis System), and others. SPSS has been translated for such small minicomputers as the HP2000 (in BASIC), and it is possible that a variation of the HP program could be written to run on a micro.

It is obvious that if we have a really large data file to analyze, we probably should still do it on a large mainframe. On the other hand, there are many statistical and numerical problems where the required data set is not overly large. A data set with a hundred variables (data elements) and 200 or 300 observations (records) can be easily contained on a typical single-sided, double-density, 5.25-inch diskette. A properly coded statistical program could be used easily to analyze such a data set provided that it was easy to use and execute. Such a program would be an asset to any comprehensive program library in a large organization.

Communicating with Other Computers

A significant proportion of this book is devoted to microcomputers within a network environment. It is quite possible that initial acquisitions of micros in a large organization will not need such communications. But if the organization has one or more mainframes, accessed interactively, then sooner or later the user of the microcomputer will need communications capabilities. As mentioned in Chapter 2, there are two basic forms of communications: asynchronous and synchronous. Most micros can communicate, using the RS232 serial port, as asynchronous terminals. Some micros such as (TRS-80 Models II and 16, the IBM Personal Computer, and the IBM Model 23 small business computer) can communicate in both modes with additional software (and sometimes hardware). The specific communications disciplines (or protocols) need not concern us here. We do need to identify the essential functional specification for appropriate software (and hardware) to be able to do adequate communications.

All mainframe computer manufacturers offering any on-line interactive communications provide for communications through a serial, RS232 standard interface. This is the simplest and cheapest way to communicate. On the microcomputer end, the micro must be equipped with an electronic interface device (standard on some machines, but relatively inexpensive when not standard). If the micro is then hard-wired, it is connected to the communications controller on the mainframe or to a modem if the distances are too great. If access is to be by dial-up phone lines, then a modem also is required. The most common transmission speed for dial-up communications is 300 baud (bits per second or 30 characters per second), although the higher 1200-baud rate was becoming more widely used, especially within large organizations, by the early 1980s. The RS232 serial interfaces placed on micros often can communicate at speeds up to 9600 baud or even 19.2 kilobaud, but most 8-bit processors cannot run fast enough to handle such speeds without some very fancy programming. The 1200-baud speed is about the highest that can be used with reliability for off-the-shelf communications programs.

The standard form of communications with IBM mainframes is with synchronous (or bisynchronous) communications using one of two protocols: 3270 (interactive) or 2780/3780 (batch) communications. Synchronous communication offers some advantages over asynchronous, including speed and other features, but at the sacrifice of higher cost. It is interesting to note that IBM's Model 23 small business computer (introduced in 1981 at the high price end of the market) came standard with both asynchronous and synchronous communications as did Radio Shack's TRS-80 Model 16 introduced early in 1982. The end user of the micro does not have the choice of communications protocols; that is a function of the network management and of decisions reached when the network is designed. In late 1981 there were only four micros provided with synchronous software and interface: the TRS-80 Models II and 16, the IBM Personal Computer, and the IBM Model 23.

The principal component for allowing a micro to talk with another computer is the communications software available for the micro. It is fairly easy and inexpensive to make the micro emulate a simple "dumb" terminal. To be useful in a dynamic manner in a large organization, however, it is necessary for the communications program to have "intelligence"—that is, it must allow the user to communicate effectively in several modes. At a bare minimum, the software must have the ability to upload data from the micro to the mainframe and to download data from the mainframe to the micro. Much of what is done on a mainframe time-sharing system consists of creating files with a text editor. Almost all such data preparation can be done offline on a micro and uploaded to the mainframe for execution.

This will obviously constitute a major savings in communications costs and in computer time charges on the mainframe. Similarly, when examining the results of the calculations done by the mainframe, it can be done at leisure if the results have been downloaded to the micro. To reiterate the example used previously, when using the electronic mail system on the central computer system with which I deal, I typically prepare the text offline on a micro and then upload the text directly into the mail system. Furthermore, if I want the document to be nicely formatted, I first run it through a text formatter which is capable of outputting formatted text to a disk file. It is this formatted file I then upload. I use a minimum of central computer time and resources and am certain that the resulting text is reasonably error-free and attractive.

Uploading usually can be accomplished with some degree of ease. Time-sharing systems must have some sort of text editing facility. Consequently, "handshaking" can take place between the micro and the mainframe by having the micro's communications software send a line and then wait for the text editor to respond with a prompt. If the mainframe's text editor does not produce a prompt, it then may be necessary to write a simple program for the mainframe that will read a line from the terminal, output it to disk, and then prompt the micro to continue. Downloading is not usually as convenient. Typically, some utility program is used to list a file, which is trapped in a large memory buffer on the micro and then saved on the micro's disk. The trouble with this approach is that some extraneous information is always transmitted at the beginning and end of the file. An alternative to this problem is to write a program on the mainframe that will read a file on the mainframe, turn on the memory buffer of the micro, download the appropriate file, turn off the memory buffer on the micro, and complete execution.

A second major feature needed in a communications program is the ability to get to the disk operating system of the micro without breaking contact with the mainframe. It is frequently necessary to use the micro's operating system (obtain file names, kill files, etc.) while in a period of dialogue with the mainframe. In fact, all the features of the micro's operating system should be available to the user from the communications program. Farther down the line in importance, but sometimes of considerable use, is the ability to access the major language of the micro (usually BASIC) while the micro and the mainframe are still in communications with one another. A helpful, though certainly not essential, feature is an ability for the micro to automatically log the user onto the central mainframe. It would also be useful, in a dial-up environment, to be able to have the micro automatically dial the host computer.

The auto-dial feature requires an appropriate modem, of course. If security is an issue (and it should be in large organizations), the micro also might be equipped with an auto-answer modem so that when communication is initially established with the mainframe, the mainframe can break the connection and dial the micro back. This feature — which requires additional hardware and software at both ends — also would provide the basics needed for automatic reception of data and mail by the micro without it being online at all times.

If there is need to access more than one computer, especially those of different manufacturers, then the communications program should have a few additional features. The ability to turn the screen echo (printing a character on the screen when a key is pressed) on and off is important, depending on whether the computer is using half duplex (IBM computers) or full duplex (virtually all others). In a half duplex system data goes in only one direction at a time, and anything typed at the terminal must be reflected on the screen by the terminal or it will be blank. In a full duplex system, the host computer reflects everything it receives back to the terminal. Consequently, if everything coming from the mainframe is printed on the terminal and the terminal also is printing (echoing) what it sends, the user will get double characters on the screen or printer. Conversely, if the terminal is in full duplex mode but operating with a half duplex computer, then nothing from the local keyboard will be echoed on the terminal. This is an issue if communications to both IBM and non-IBM machines is necessary — not an infrequent occurrence in large organizations. Other useful features include the ability to control a printer, to alter the video display mode, and to reinitialize the RS232 interface to different characteristics (again, useful if more than one time-sharing system is to be used).

There are off-the-shelf communications packages that offer most of the features noted above. In fact, a few micros come with such communications packages as standard (the TRS-80 Model II, for example). One excellent example of a fairly complete communications package is the ST80 series (by Lance Micklus, Inc.). That program, which operates on a TRS-80

Model I and Model II, provides almost all the features mentioned with the exception of the auto dial/auto answer and a few others. Other software packages have been advertised that claim essentially the same features as those found in the ST80 for a wide variety of machines. Several communications programs are also available at a very low cost as part of the CP/M Users Group library. If a large organization were to invest heavily in micros, it would probably be cost-effective to assign a programmer to produce a tailored communications package that would make explicit use of the micros acquired as well as take explicit advantage of the mainframe's capabilities. This would enable the organization to integrate the uploading and downloading capabilities on the micros with the format of data produced by the mainframe. More will be said of this later.

Data Collection and Control

The primary meaning of "data collection" in this context is automated data collection — the capturing of data from some automated process. Likewise, "data control" also means the control of automated processes. Having said this, I will hasten to add that some data collection efforts may involve human intervention as may some data control efforts. To the extent that we are talking about data collection with substantial amounts of human intervention, this area crosses with the data management issues discussed above. This is equally true of the data control process. To the extent that data collection and control are automatic by-products of some process, however, we are really addressing additional uses of the microcomputer.

If they are equipped with the appropriate data entry programs, micros can be powerful intelligent data entry stations for operators. Essentially what we are talking about here is a one-for-one replacement of keypunches (which produce punched cards) with microcomputer devices. Clearly, when using micros for this purpose the communications function is important if the data are ultimately intended for use on a mainframe computer. Somewhat related to this kind of function would be the validation of complex job streams to be uploaded to a mainframe and run in a batch environment. In fact, it would be possible to create a job control language (JCL) scanner on the micro that would evaluate and verify the job stream and report any error to an operator. Again, the objective is to do off-line whatever can be done efficiently and effectively and not impact either the mainframe itself or its attached communications system.

Within large organizations the control of production, laboratory, or other processes can be an important, if specialized function. In addition, many parts of a large computing system also must be monitored and controlled, and errors must be logged. Forms of social and financial data also can be automatically collected as a by-product of other efforts, such as point-of-sale functions. In all these applications there is a major role for microcomputers. If we are talking about the control of specific machines, such as a lathe, the micro would be a special-purpose system designed for numerical control. On the other hand, virtually all the other functions mentioned above can be performed by general-purpose micros. Allied to such functions (in concept and logic if not in purpose) are security control systems (such as monitoring doors, locks, and related devices).

For some production processes, and for a number of laboratory processes, general-purpose microcomputers can be used to watch and monitor data collection changes or can respond with changes in the event the data reach (or fail to reach) some threshold or another. Several manufacturerers of computer communications devices (often called port selectors or contenders), such as Develcon (who produces the "Dataswitch") or Gandalf, specifically provide for an administrator's terminal which can collect, on a diskette, information concerning the performance of the communication system. This terminal is a general, not special, purpose micro. Similarly, micros can be attached to mainframes to capture or monitor performance information so that the mainframe can be tuned appropriately.

Micros that are more special purpose may be used for point-of-sales systems, although standard micros also could serve the function. The key element here is that such systems, connected in a local area network, could capture related financial and inventory information for use by the management of the retail systems. This enables automatic ordering and other aspects of inventory control. Such point-of-sales systems can be either part of a network or stand-alone systems designed to make records of transactions on tape or disk. The output medium is physically transported to some central site for analysis, and summarization is done either by another more general-purpose micro system or by a large mainframe. Similarly, intelligent security systems can monitor activity through the system, checking (with the appropriate input devices) whether an individual has authorized access and collecting data on traffic patterns to improve the system.

On the whole, the software for applications such as those noted either must be written locally or must come as a package as part of a security system or a point-of-sale system. These are not the kinds of applications for which one can produce (at least not easily) off-the-shelf software at low cost. The control functions associated with the communications devices, by way of contrast, can be used with standard micros and standard software. Moreover, as standard, off-the-shelf, local area network software becomes available, and as low-cost network-connecting devices are developed, we may see more standard software written for such activities as security control. Certainly the hardware for performing most of these functions is rather easily available, and sooner or later a good bit of software is likely to follow.

Some Other Interesting Applications

Some of the uses to which microcomputers are being put are specialized versions of one or another of the applications already mentioned. Captain Grace M. Hopper has reported at several lectures that at least some of the programmers for the Department of the Navy have been equipped with micros next to their terminals. The purpose of the micros is to provide an immediate method for documenting the programs being developed online to a large system. When the program is finished, the documentation also is largely finished. The only thing needed on the micro is a word processing system.

A related use is as a programmer's work station in a large-scale computer programming staff. In such an environment program code can be entered and edited, and perhaps even initial compiles can be run before the programmer has need to access the central system. Because each programmer would be using a stand-alone micro for most preliminary purposes, the cost in computer time (which can extend to thousands of dollars for just the preliminary efforts) itself could pay for the system. By late 1981 there were a number of micros coming on the market that could routinely address as much as 256K (256 times 1024) bytes of memory. The typical region size accessible to a programmer on even large mainframes is normally not more than that amount. The point is that it is possible to do a good bit of initial development on a stand-alone micro, and then, with the appropriate communications software, upload to the large machines for final testing and production.

THE MANAGER'S WORK STATION

Much of what has been said in this chapter resolves itself into the concept of the "manager's work station." This simply means having a device available for the manager (middle level, upper level, lower level, or whatever) that allows this person to be more productive for the organization. An ideal work station would provide the ability to do text editing and formatting, communications, planning and analysis, project control, and whatever other managerial problems might be faced in the particular industry involved. Such a work station also would have utilities for keeping track of schedules, calendars, notes on various topics, and perhaps an automated tickle file so that important matters would not be overlooked.

I wish I could say that an integrated set of software and hardware was already available to provide an off-the-shelf manager's work station—but this is not the case. On the other hand, almost all the software, and quite likely all the hardware, is available for constructing such a work station. It possible to put the software together in a way that is easily accessible and friendly to the user. The development of such a system cannot be left to a computer novice, but if you happen to fall into that category, you should now know that all the basics do, in fact, exist. To acquire a comprehensive manager's work station, it may be necessary to have some programming done, and it may be necessary to obtain some direction and consultation from outside your organization. Large data processing centers do not (yet) typically have personnel with the skills needed to put together an integrated microcomputer package of the sort I have described. The cost of such a work station, however, is well within the limits of many large organizations and can be purchased for considerably less than $10,000. The mid-1980s will certainly see many more developments in the directions indicated, and they will come about with or without conscious planning. In Chapter 4 we will explore some ways in which the work station concept can be implemented.

Designing a
Manager's Work Station

One of the major potential uses for microcomputers in large organizations is as a manager's work station. This chapter will provide a demonstration of how such a work station might be designed primarily with off-the-shelf software and hardware. The examples and associated utility programs are structured around a TRS-80 Model III micro from Radio Shack, although somewhat equivalent systems could be designed around CP/M-based systems. When appropriate, an attempt will be made to specifically illustrate how one function or another might be implemented on systems running under CP/M as well as those running under TRSDOS.

The point of this chapter is not to promote particular hardware or software but to demonstrate how a manager's work station might be structured with a minimum number of problems. As will be seen, a few simple programs must be written in order to provide a fully integrated system. These programs, which consist of a few utility and applications programs, are listed at the end of the chapter. Although this chapter is more technical than others in this book, it provides an explicit illustration of what was possible in the early 1980s. To implement a full manager's work station, as described here, it would be helpful to obtain the assistance of a programmer or other technically qualified person.

DESIGN CONSIDERATIONS AND ASSUMPTIONS

One of the major advantages of using microcomputers as a manager's work station is that as such it can be tailored to the needs of the individual. Nevertheless, there are some assumptions that *should* be made concerning the operating system environment and the specific list of software to be included. We are emphasizing the ability to establish a work station based on off-the-shelf software, so the first consideration is that appropriate software be available without the need for extensive programming. The software issues fall into three categories: operating system capabilities, applications software for the specific individual need, and associated utility programs required to make the entire system function in a simple, straightforward, and friendly manner. We need to consider these categories with some care.

Operating System Capabilities

Regardless of whether we are talking about a TRS-80 or about some other microcomputer system, there are a number of operating systems available. An operating system is a program that manages other programs. In addition, based on the capabilities of the particular operating system, there will be several associated utility programs. A utility program is a program that assists the user in doing repetitive general-purpose procedures. Almost all systems, for example, have a "copy" program which allows the copying of disk files from one disk to another — such a program is called a utility. The Disk Operating System (DOS) normally distributed with a TRS-80 is called TRSDOS and is manufactured and marketed by Radio Shack. There are several TRSDOS-compatible DOSs manufactured and marketed by others, such as LDOS (by Logical Systems, Inc.), NEWDOS/80 (by Apparat), and DOSPLUS (by Micro Systems Software). Each DOS offers its own set of bells and whistles. In addition, several vendors supply versions of CP/M for the TRS-80 series. CP/M (Control Program for Microcomputers) is a very widely used DOS available for a large number of micros and is probably the most widely used DOS in general business-oriented micro systems.

What convenience should a DOS possess in order to provide the appropriate operating enivironment for a manager's work/station? At least the following:

1. *A Command Processor.* A "command processor" provides the user with a facility for building a file of DOS commands (including the names of application programs) that will be executed sequentially and automatically by issuing a single command from the keyboard. In its original incarnation on the Model I, TRSDOS did not have such a facility. Both the Models II and III TRSDOS can use a "DO" file (created with the BUILD command) which, when executed, in turn will execute all the commands in the DO file. The TRSDOS version is relatively primitive compared to some of the other DOSs (and the three compatible DOSs mentioned above have more extensive facilities), but it is useful and workable. Under CP/M systems the SUBMIT command is used for the same purpose and accesses a file of commands in a manner similar to the DO statement in the other DOSs. The format for the two commands is DO filename/BLD or SUBMIT filename. SUB. In building an integrated or "turnkey" system, this facility is *very* important.

2. *An AUTO start feature.* Although this feature is less important than a command processor, it also is useful for turnkey systems. An AUTO start facility provides a means for automatically executing a program or command file immediately after the computer is turned on. For a manager's work station, this means that after the computer is reset and the work station diskette is placed in the machine, a master menu program immediately will provide a choice of programs, one of which is to be used. Although not an absolute requirement, this feature contributes to the implementation of a turnkey system. The TRSDOS-oriented DOSs all have an AUTO feature, and an AUTO start feature can be added to CP/M systems, although this may require some additional programming.

Applications Software

Of even greater importance than the particular DOS is the availability of appropriate applications software. What is "appropriate" depends, of course, on the particular use to which the work station is to be put. For a general-purpose manager's work station we identified several items in Chapter 3, a word processing package, a computational planning and modeling package, an "intelligent" communications program, and a data management program. Other possible programs include a general note-taking facility and an appointments calendar.

One of the problems that must be met in doing a design for a work station is not only the simple availability of the appropriate software, but also the ability to copy and move the software from one disk to another. Because of an implicit "black market" in microcomputer software, many software publishers and manufacturers are resorting to various safeguards that limit the ability to copy or backup programs. The Model III versions of SCRIPSIT and VISICALC distributed by Radio Shack in 1981 illustrate this point. Those software packages were protected to limit the number of backups to two, and no independent copies could be made (although one independent software house did produce a program which circumvented the protective devices used). Consequently, without overriding the security locks on the software, it is difficult to combine the various pieces of software on a single disk (or two). The point is, marketing strategies of vendors may have to be assessed before a final selection of software is made.

Another problem that may complicate the design of a compact work station system is the sheer size of one or more items of software. That is, it may not be possible to put a word processor, a spreadsheet program, and a communications program all on the same diskette. The decisions made concerning the selection of software may (and probably should) influence such hardware decisions as the number of disk drives to acquire initially as well as the particular computer to buy. It also may be necessary to cut out some features of a system to make it fit with the other software, although a full system disk should be available for complete coverage. An example of this is NEWSCRIPT's system for handling the production of indexes. The actual printing and formatting of indexes is done by a separate program from their version of SCRIPT. Since this is an infrequently used feature, however, the index compilation program may be safely purged from the work-station disk although a full word processing disk would retain it for needed applications.

All the application software mentioned for inclusion in the work station system require output disk files of varying sizes. Any such files should be put on disks other than the work station system disk (although some small work files may have to reside on the system disk). On a two-disk system it likely that the data diskettes would have to be changed for each application. Perhaps the ideal hardware configuration, using 5.25-inch double density disks, would be four disk drives with one being used for the system, the second for word processing files, the third for spreadsheet files, and the fourth for files dealing with notes and calendars. While this might represent one kind of "ideal" configuration, the fact is that only one application disk can be used at a time, and it does not represent much effort to make the diskette changes.

The third major component of the manager's work station is the communications program. Chapter 3 described the features such a program should possess. An intelligent communications program also will require some disk space in addition to that needed for the storage of the program. In the case of the communications program, auxiliary disk space requirements will not be very extensive, and it is most convenient to have such files reside on the work station system disk. Other applications programs (such as a note-taking facility, a data management program, and an appointments calendar) also will require files, but these files almost certainly will be on disks other than the system disk.

One of the design considerations might be whether the initial program run after the computer is turned on should be a menu program for the entire system or an appointments calendar that would automatically report the requirements for the day. Another possible alternative is an automatic log on to the user's mainframe computer with an automatic execution of the internal electronic mail system. The latter approach immediately would display any messages that had arrived since the user had previously read his/her mail. Some of these considerations may be a matter of personal taste, or a matter of the work style and work demands of the individual manager. A comprehensive work station design should make such features optional to the user.

Associated Utility Programs

As mentioned above, utility programs are those which allow the user to complete repetitive tasks with a minimum of time and effort. There are operating system utilities, programming utilities, and utilities for specialized systems. For a work station design only a few utilities are necessary, but they should be regarded as necessary rather than merely desirable.

Such utilities include a menu program which displays the components of the system and allows the user the option of selecting whatever component is needed at the moment. Generally, after the execution of any given component, the system should return to the master menu. If the system has an attached "smart" printer (one with variable type fonts, spacing features, or other attributes), then there should be a utility that allows the user to set the features of the printer without going outside the system. Frequently it is necessary to be able to display the disk directory for any diskette currently online. Most operating systems allow for directory displays, but the work station user should be able to do this from the work station system. Finally, there should be some way (and these should be menu items on the master menu) for the user to escape the system to the DOS or to BASIC (or the major language processor).

The Work Station—
A Systematic Overview

In Figure 1 the entire work station concept has been summarized in a diagram. Upon entry to the system the user should be presented with a simple, easy-to-understand menu of options. Those options should be, at

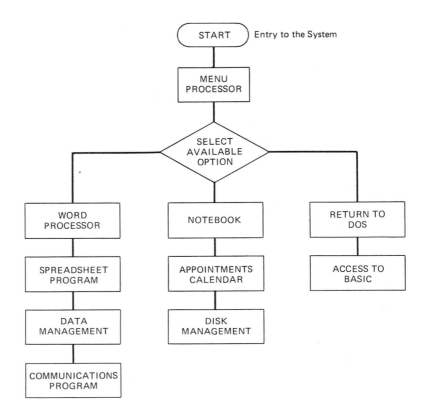

a minimum, nine in number: (1) a word processor (2) a spreadsheet program (3) a data management system (4) a communications program (5) a notebook program (6) an appointments calendar (7) disk management (8) a return to DOS and (9) an access to BASIC (or other major language processor). The latter, of course, could be optional, depending on the specific user but the escape to the DOS should be mandatory.

There may be routes to at least two additional submenus: one for word processing and one for disk management. Although we have not discussed this point previously, it should be considered. Depending on use, it may be necessary to provide more than one word processing system. The reason for this is that while in the early 1980s there were a number of good and powerful word processing packages on the market, there was no one system that contained all the "bells" and "whistles" one might need. I routinely use three word processors: SCRIPSIT, NEWSCRIPT, and a homegrown system.

SCRIPSIT is useful for "quick and dirty" word processing. NEWSCRIPT is useful for complex manuscripts, such as this book. The home-grown system provides features the others lack, such as automatic formatting of various disk files. For example, if I want to send a neatly formatted message over my electronic mail system, I first edit it with EDIT under NEWSCRIPT. I then format it with our home-grown formatter, which places the formatted text on a diskette. I then enter the communications program and directly upload the formatted message into the mail system. The home-grown formatter also produces formatted comment statements for both BASIC and FORTRAN, as well as files of PRINT or DATA statements for BASIC programs, thus allowing neat internal documentation for programmers. Examples of these features may be seen in the program listings at the end of this chapter.

As noted in Figure 1, a similar situation can exist with respect to disk management. For a complete work station it should be possible for the user to do some disk management without exiting to the DOS. Specifically, it should be possible for the user to look at a directory of any on-line disk, kill files, rename files, or do whatever other file management task is desirable. While the larger programs in the system (wordprocessing, spreadsheet, and communications) are generally available as off-the-shelf items, other features of the system may not be so easily acquired. Later in this chapter illustrative programs in BASIC are presented by which this system can be implemented. I must stress, however, that in a normal working environment it might be better to implement the supporting programs in a compiled language rather than with a BASIC interpreter to improve the speed of access, although I suspect that this may not be a major problem.

You may recall from the discussion in Chapter 3 that there are other software packages an individual user might find helpful or necessary. A financial planner, for example, might find that less emphasis on one facet of the work station (word processing, for example) is desirable along with more emphasis on analytical and statistical systems. Consequently, instead of showing one box for analysis, we might have shown another submenu for analytical procedures that included a spreadsheet program along with frequently used analytical or statistical programs. How elaborate the system becomes is, to a great extent, a function of the disk space available. Our present objective is to demonstrate that an extremely useful manager's work station can be implemented around two double-density, 40-track, 5.25-inch disk drives simply because in the early 1980s that configuration was rapidly becoming an off-the-shelf standard. However, if we are willing to go to somewhat "nonstandard" hardware configurations (double-density, 80-track drives, for example), then we would be able to design a much more elaborate work station.

IMPLEMENTING THE WORK STATION

The guiding principle in the selection of microcomputer hardware for any purpose always should be the availability of appropriate software. (More will be said of this in Chapter 5.) At this point, it is necessary to delineate a minimum hardware configuration for a manager's work station and the features it must possess. We already have discussed disk drives and we will expand on that below. In addition to disk drives we also must have a screen large enough to do useful work. The third element of a minimal work station must be a usable keyboard. Once we have defined the minimal hardware configuration, we can take a closer look at how a work station might be implemented on a specific microcomputer system.

Hardware Configuration

The Disk Drives.   The minimum useful configuration for the disk drives would be two double-density, 40-track, 5.25-inch, floppy drives. There are a number of other possibilities that can be acquired for most major microcomputer systems, although very few come standard with such drives. Examples of other possibilities are two double-density, 80-track drives; one double-density, 40-track drive; 5-megabyte Winchester drive; two 8-inch floppy disk drives; or some combination of these. In addition, as we already noted, for specific applications it might be worthwhile to acquire more than two drives. Most microcomputer systems can handle at least four drives and, for a specific work station, more than two drives may be desirable at the beginning. Single-density, 35 or 40-track drives (such as those sold with the old TRS-80 Model I, the original versions of the Osborne 1, and some other micros) simply do not have sufficient storage capabilities to adequately implement the work-station concept. Osborne, for example, after the initial introduction of the Osborne 1, came out with a double-density option. A number of independent manufacturers produce a wide variety of disk options for the TRS-80 series, APPLE, and other popular microcomputers.

Screen Size.   The minimal screen size for a work station must be large enough for word processing. The normal typed letter or manuscript typically has a line length of 6 inches. When the text is printed on a printer with a common type style having 10 characters per inch (pica type on a typewriter), the line length is 60 characters. The screen also must have sufficient additional character space per line to account for any control fields used by the word processor. This means that the minimal line length for the video display is about 64 characters. The standard APPLE·II display of 40 characters is clearly inadequate, and providing an 80-character display runs the price up. An alternative approach is the Osborne 1.

The Osborne has a line display length of 52 characters, but it automatically scrolls left and right for a total line length of 128 characters. Consequently, the Osborne screen can be used adequately for most work station purposes. (The manuscript for this chapter, in fact, was written on an Osborne, although the rest of the book was written on a TRS-80 Model III. This text was transferred to the Model III for final printing because the text was structured for NEWSCRIPT rather than for WORDSTAR.) The screen also must display a sufficient number lines so that a comprehensible amount of information can be on the screen at any one time. The TRS-80 Model III probably possesses the minimal usable screen size: 64 characters by 16 lines. Industry standard terminals, by the way, use 80-character by 24-line displays. Some word processing systems use a 60-70 line display to simulate a full typed page of paper.

The Keyboard.   Although this may not seem to be an important item, the keyboard and its layout can be important to the person using the work station many hours a day. In general the keyboard should have a typewriter style in standard QWERTY format. In addition, it is helpful if there are several additional keys such as four arrow keys for the control of the cursor (and for other specialized functions). There also should be a capital lock key, a control key, and a numeric keypad in addition to the standard typewriter keys. Of course, the device must be capable of generating both capital and lowercase characters.

The tactile response of the keyboard (including the possibility of auditory feedback if a silent keyboard is used) is also an important consideration. If it is necessary to pound heavily on the keyboard (as with old manual typewriters), people will not use the machine with any degree of ease. Some of these considerations make the use of a TRS-80 Model III marginal, although the Model II possesses the appropriate configuration. In addition, the availability of programmable function keys also can enhance the usefulness of the system. On the Model III, the control key function is accessed by concurrently pressing the shift and down-arrow keys, and the capital lock is simulated by pressing the shift and the zero key.

Other Hardware Considerations.   There are a few other hardware considerations implicit in what was said previously. First, the system must have communications ports. That is, it must be configured with an RS232 serial port and/or a (bi)synchronous communications port. It also must have the ability to communicate with a printer through something other than the RS232 port. In the early 1980s the latter consideration meant having a "Centronics"-type parallel printer port available. A work station need not necessarily always have a printer attached to it (although most people find it desirable), but it must have the ability to produce printed copy when necessary. If the work station is to be used by people who travel frequently, it is mandatory that the computer be designed for easy portability. In late 1981 the most easily available system so configured was the Osborne 1.

An Illustrative
Hardware/Software Configuration

For illustrative purposes we will demonstrate how a manager's work station might be implemented on a TRS-80 Model III microcomputer. This particular piece of hardware is chosen because it represents the minimal hardware configuration for such a work station. Any number of other computers would do at least as well, and many would be more suitable. Vector Graphic, IBM, Xerox, Radio Shack, and a host of others produce equipment eminently suitable for this application. All these, however, are more costly. For a somewhat more specialized work station, an Osborne 1 also might have been chosen. The purpose of this section is not to promote specific computer equipment or software but to give an explicit example of how the work station concept can be implemented. It is easy to recommend a maximum system for almost anything. It is much more difficult, however, to demonstrate how a more or less minimal configuration can be used to produce a useful, usable system. For this reason I am using the TRS-80 Model III as the sample system.

Selecting the Hardware.   The microcomputer consists of Radio Shack's so-called business system configuration for the Model III. The system has a 48K (49, 152, alpha numeric characters since K equals 1024) user memory plus an additional 16K dedicated memory for a total of 64K. It is configured with two double-density, 40-track, 5.25-inch disk drives (built into an integrated cabinet). It comes standard with a Centronics parallel printer port, an RS232 serial port, and a disk connector for two additional disk drives. The screen size, as noted above, is a minimal 64 characters by 16 lines, and the character generator produces both capital and lowercase letters as well as providing some (rough) graphics capabilities. The keyboard has some good features including good tactile response and a numeric keypad. However, there is no independent control key or independent capital lock key, although these functions are provided through the use of a combination of other keys. The Model III lacks any auditory response capability; there is no "bell" when [CONTROL]G is pressed. The latter capability is present on most industrial quality terminals and can be handy when it is necessary to signal the user. When implemented with a text editor the bell also can be used much like the bell on a typewriter to signal the end of a line.

Although not strictly necessary, it also is appropriate to include a printer in the repertoire of hardware. A quality word processing printer must use one of three technologies to produce output: the IBM Selectric mechanism, the Diablo Daisywheel system, or the NEC thimble device. There are, however, some excellent quality matrix printers available for micros that can produce very acceptable copy for word processing situations. The matrix printers cost one-third to one-fourth (or even less) as much as the higher quality printers and, for the majority of work internal to an organization, are suitable for most applications. In addition, many of the matrix printers run at speeds well above those of the Selectric/Daisywheel/ thimble arrangements. Two of the best quality matrix printers producing proportional spacing and descenders (characters with tails which fall below the line of type such as "y" or "p") are the Centronics 737 (Radio Shack Lineprinter IV) and the Centronics 739 (Radio Shack Lineprinter VIII). These printers can also print 132 characters on an 8-inch line. A 132-character line is the traditional line length for most data processing applications.

A final hardware component involves the selection of a device that allows communications with a larger system. This is the modem mentioned in Chapter 2. A modem is necessary when the distance between the microcomputer (being used as a terminal) and the attached computer is in excess of several hundred feet, or when communications are to take place via dial-up telephone lines. If the mainframe computer is relatively close, and if the host computer system is so structured, direct connections between the terminal and mainframe may be possible. In general it would be best to communicate at as high a speed as possible, although many dial-up networks operate at the relatively slow speed of 300 baud (bits per second—about 30 alphanumeric characters per second). An advantage is that the 300 baud modems are relatively inexpensive, both at the user's end and at the host computer's site.

For dial-up purposes there are two types of modems on the market: acoustic couplers, which possess a cradle into which the telephone handset is inserted, and direct connect modems, which plug directly into a modular jack on the telephone line. At the low-cost end acoustic couplers and direct connect modems operating at 300 baud cost about $150. Most of the direct-connect modems possess the ability to originate communications (as do all acoustic couplers) as well as to answer calls originated elsewhere. With the low-priced modems, however, a human being must be present to press a button or flip a switch. Somewhat more expensive direct-connect modems (in the $300 range) provide for auto-dial and auto-answer features that allow unattended operation. The move to 1200-baud communications generally represents a leap of several times the price of 300-baud modems (to the $600 to $1200 range). Many communications software packages on micros do not work well at baud rates greater than 1200 even though they can be set to run at higher speeds. If lines are laid by an organization, or are leased from the telephone company, and are used for permanent installations, somewhat different types of modems are available. Local area netwoks often require a specialized modem or other specialized equipment.

An Appropriate Software Configuration.   To reiterate a point made on several previous occasions, there are at least six software items that would be useful to the work station: a word processor, a computational spreadsheet program, a data management program, a communications package, a note-taking program, and an appointments calendar. There are others, of course, which might fit a particular circumstance, but those mentioned are the most frequently used programs. One appropriate list of software, which can be placed on a single 5.25-inch diskette (using double density), is the following:

1. NEWSCRIPT from PROSOFT. This (Waterloo or IBM) SCRIPT and EDITOR look-alike is a flexible editor/formatter combination for general word processing. It will properly drive several proportional spacing printers such as the Centronics 739 or the Radio Shack Lineprinter VIII. Some minor modifications must be made to the program (a task made relatively easy since the programs are written largely in BASIC) so that when processing is completed, the operating system will be recalled. This is necessary because NEWSCRIPT, like most word processors, takes over the system rather completely. Before continuing with other tasks, it is necessary to either press the reset button or to accomplish the equivalent function within the program. The documentation is good and complete.

2. VISICALC from Personal Software and marketed for the TRS-80 series by Radio Shack. This is one of several speadsheet programs available on the market for the TRS-80 series as well as for other micros. It also is one of the better such programs and typically comes with quite good documentation, an issue that should not be overlooked. Because it comes from Radio Shack, the program is protected so that it cannot be backed up more than twice and cannot be copied at all. In order to integrate the package into a work-

station disk, it is necessary to violate these security protections or to place the other programs on a VISICALC diskette. The purpose of the limitations on copying is to protect the copyrights of Personal Software and Radio Shack. On the other hand, it makes the program considerably less useful in a context such as the work station. Consequently, one of the other spreadsheet programs already mentioned might be more accessible. At least one vendor sells a program to remove the security locks from both the VISICALC and SCRIPSIT disks.

3. PROFILE from Radio Shack (Tandy). Although there are a number of data management packages available, PROFILE has received generally good reviews, is well documented, and is easily available (and moderately priced). It does not have any security locks to prevent copying and, as a consequence, can be easily integrated into a work-station package. It provides the ability to create, modify, and retrieve files and has the added advantage of producing output files that can be read by other programs written in BASIC.

4. ST80III from Lance Micklus, Inc. ST80III is an excellent communications package for the Model III. It contains most of the functions noted earlier. It runs well at either 300 or 1200 baud, although the documentation indicates that the user may encounter some difficulties at higher baud rates. I have had no problems running the program at 1200 baud. There are no software or hardware security features that prevent copying, so this package, like NEWSCRIPT and PROFILE, can be integrated easily on a work-station diskette.

5. A Notebook Program (locally produced). Although there may be such programs on the market now, at the end of 1981 there were none that would run easily under TRSDOS or TRSDOS-like operating systems. PERCOM provided an illustrative notebook program of the general sort needed on their BASIC-oriented operating system (OS-80). Using the PERCOM NOTEBOOK program under TRSDOS requires extensive rewriting, and some additional "bells" and "whistles" are needed to make the program really effective. Listing 1 at the end of this chapter provides such a rewrite of the PERCOM NOTEBOOK program. It is probably better to suggest that the NOTEBOOK program in Listing 1 was inspired by the PERCOM program rather than a modification of the earlier software. The program when run is self-explanatory and contains a HELP file that explains the various commands.

6. An Appointments Calendar (locally produced). Although Tandy announced a time management program late in 1981, and others are being advertised, such a program is provided here. The program presented in Listing 2 at the end of this chapter was inspired by an article in 80-MICROCOMPUTING although, like the notebook program, the originally published program was modified so extensively that it is a new program for all practical purposes. Also like the notebook program, the appointments calendar is relatively self-explanatory and contains a HELP file that explains each command.

7. A Disk Management Program (locally produced). A program that reads the disk directory of any disk online and then allows some limited manipulation of the files is presented in Listing 3. The program in Listing 3 at the end of this chapter was inspired by a published program in *TRS-80 Microcomputer News* (August 1981), published by Tandy. The program first reads the disk directory indicated and then provides the user with the capacity to "kill" (erase) a file, copy a file, or "execute" (start the operation of) any appropriate file. It does these tasks by turning the directory into an extended menu. The user then chooses which function to perform and enters the number of the file to manipulated. The program does the rest.

8. A Menu Program (locally produced). The MENU program provided in Listing 4 at the end of this chapter represents an example of a general-purpose menu-producing program. Note that there are several "DATA" statements at the end of the program. Without getting into what a DATA statement is, simply rest assured that those statements provide two items of information to the program (each of the items is enclosed in double quotes): the name of the program or disk file to be executed (or system command) and an English description of the function. The DATA statement with the "/*" must always remain, because it tells the program when it has run out of data. Simply by changing the DATA statements (changing the content and/or number of statements) one automatically produces properly paged and formatted menus. The general-purpose menu program is required to integrate the system, as can be seen in Figure 1.

The locally produced programs are all written in standard Microsoft (TRS-80) interpreter BASIC for the sake of clarity and transportability. When actually constructing a work station diskette, it might be better (and certainly faster) to rewrite these programs so that they can be compiled (translated into machine language). There are several BASIC compilers available on the market that could be used for this purpose, or they could be rewritten in such languages as COBOL or FORTRAN. These off-the-shelf software items, along with the BASIC language programs provided, allow the construction of a minimal work station on a TRS-80 Model III. Much the same sort of system could be structured on a CP/M system. Equivalent software is available for CP/M systems, and the BASIC programs could be adapted. In addition to the programs noted or listed above, some simple operating system-level functions have to be invoked.

To make the system a "turnkey" package (one automatically invoked for the user), a "DO" file would have to be built using the BUILD command which would contain one line: BASIC MENU/BAS. The AUTO command would have to be used to automatically invoke the DO file following the starting of the machine. Several other short DO files also would be useful. For example, VISICALC when exited does not do a "cold start" — it does not restart the operating system. Consequently, it is possible to simply issue the command DO MENU when VISICALC returns the user to TRSDOS (or other DOS), automatically invoking the menu program. On the other hand, the user may want to go immediately to one of the other programs in the system (the notebook program, for example). Consequently, it also would be useful if all the user had to do was to type DO NOTEBOOK instead of invoking BASIC and then issuing the command RUN NOTEBOOK/BAS.

Notes on Copying Software. We have mentioned that several software packages, such as VISICALC, seek to prevent the user from making excessive copies of the programs. The primary reason software vendors have started resorting to such techniques is that software is typically licensed to a single system. In order to make money the vendor either must prevent piracy of the software (the copying of the software for individual gain or for other purposes) through limiting the number of times the software may be copied, or must not allow any copying, or must rely on the protection of the copyright. Some vendors use a combination of techniques. The suggestions made in this chapter are not designed to suggest that unlimited copies of software be made. If your organization buys two machines for the same function, then buy two copies of the appropriate software or make special arrangements with the vendor for expanded copying privileges. In order to produce integrated systems, such as the manager's work station described in this chapter, it must be possible to copy programs to a central disk, however. As a result, one criterion for purchase might be whether the software can be appropriately copied.

SELECTING A SYSTEM

The TRS-80 system used for illustration in the preceding section constitutes a minimal system appropriate for a manager's work station in terms of both price and performance. Its list price (at the end of 1981) — including the two disks, 48K, TRS-80 Model III, an auto-answer/auto-dial modem, a Radio Shack Lineprinter VIII, and all the off-the-shelf software — is about $4,080. The base computer system runs about $2500 list price, although Tandy provides some quantity and educational discount. Prices for the software are also somewhat less for the Model III than they would be for the more expensive Model II or for a CP/M-based machine. However, many of the other alternatives provide more memory, more disk storage, a larger display screen, or other important features.

An Osborne 1 computer system, given the software package that comes with the system, plus an optional monitor and optional 80 column screen display, will run about the same price as the Model III-based system once a modem and communications software have been added. For any of the commonly available systems, it also would be necessary to commit one to two weeks of a programmer's time to the project to structure the work station in a usable and friendly manner. Some of the following material is based upon an excellent unpublished paper by Gregory A. Marks entitled "Microcomputers: Basic Choice Factors" (Ann Arbor, Michigan ICPSR, The University of Michigan, 1981).

Other Hardware
Alternatives Reviewed

Apple.   The Apple II is a flexible and widely used system (estimates indicate that by 1981 some 250,000 units had been sold). As sold by Apple, however, the Apple II has a keyboard that is poorly suited to a normal production environment, has a 40-character screen which is inappropriate for any complicated work, and does not possess capital and lower-case letters on the display. In order to remedy some of its defects (though by no means all) it is necessary to acquire boards or modifications that extend the Apple II capabilities from vendors other than Apple (although these products are often available from Apple dealers.)

By the time all the appropriate hardware has been added (a board for communications, a board for an 80-column by 24-line screen display, additional memory, disk drives, and so forth), the basic hardware package is in the $4000 range before the purchase of most of the appropriate software. And there was no remedy for the inadequate keyboard in late 1981. (Apple was reported to be working on a lower cost replacement for the Apple II for introduction in 1982.) The Apple III was a newer system intended to hit the business market with many more capabilities than the Apple II. Early production problems with the Apple III, along with a lack of software, produced limited sales. The Apple II, like the TRS-80 Model III, reserves memory in ROM (read-only memory) and can have only up to 48K of user memory. The Apple III, on the other hand, can address up to 128K. The Apples are based on the 6502 microprocessors.

Radio Shack.   Because the Model III was used as an illustrative unit in earlier sections of this chapter, it is not necessary to further detail the advantages and disadvantages. The Model II is a somewhat more powerful version of the Model III, possessing an 80-column by 24-line display. Virtually no space is reserved in ROM (read-only memory) on the Model II, thus allowing more complete use of the memory of the computer. In the Model III the first 16K of memory is reserved for the operating system and BASIC in ROM. Hence the BASIC language is always resident in the system whether it is needed or not. The base price for a workable Model II hardware system is in excess of $4000. The Model II, like the Model III, is Z80-based. CP/M also is available from independent vendors for the Model II.

In a larger scale production environment the Model II is a competitive alternative to other, similarly priced machines. Because of its Z80-based architecture, the maximum amount of memory available (from Radio Shack) is 64K. More than 300,000 units of the various TRS-80 models (I, II, III, and their color computer) have been sold. Apple and Radio Shack, at the end of 1981, had captured over 50 percent of the microcomputer market. Early in 1982 Tandy announced the TRS-80 Model 16, a 16-bit microprocessor based on Motorola's 68000 chip. The unit also possessed a Z80 chip, and the entire system was upward compatible from the Model II.

One of the interesting design considerations of the Model 16 is the Z80 chip that makes it possible for the user to switch back and forth from the 8-bit processor to the 16-bit processor. This ability makes it possible for the Model 16 to run all Model II software. The base system, which initially sold for $4999, contained a standard 128K bytes of memory, upgradable to 512 bytes, and two 8-inch, double-density disk drives. The price is about equal to a fully configured Apple III or IBM personal computer but also can compete effectively with IBM's System 23, which has a low-end price of about $10,000. Communications ports standard on the Model 16, like the System 23, include both asynchronous and bisynchronous capabilities.

IBM.   IBM announced its first personal computer in late 1981. It was based on 8088 chip and uses an operating system similar to CP/M, with a full CP/M announced at the same time. The hardware was well thought out, but the lack of software for the system initially put it at a competitive disadvantage. Estimates indicated, based on the IBM name, that some 100,000 units would be sold during the first year. The 8088 is a 16-bit chip, which simply means that for some applications it will execute a program somewhat faster than an 8-bit processor and can address larger amounts of memory. Although IBM announced some software for the system, substantial amounts of off-the-shelf software is not expected until the mid-1980s, or until CP/M becomes the accepted operating system. As of late 1981 it probably was not possible to design a complete work station around the IBM personal computer, although that certainly will be remedied. The cost of a usable hardware system for a manager's work station was in the mid-$4000 range.

Commodore.   Along with the Apple and TRS-80 (Models I and III), Commodore was the third-ranking producer of micros in the early 1980s. Commodore's early entry was the PET, which competed with the minimum Apple and TRS-80 systems using cassette tapes rather than disks. In its early efforts Commodore was somewhat disorganized, and its sales suffered to some extent. Later Commodore announced a number of new products, including its renamed CBM line which is targeted to business users. The BM line uses an 80-by-24 display and has standard keyboards.

Potpourri of Integrated Systems.   In the early 1980s a number of major manufacturers (including Zenith/Heath, Xerox, NEC, DEC, Wang, and Hewlett-Packard) introduced a number of micros in the $4000 to $6000-price range. Most of these systems use CP/M as the basic operating system but Zenith/Heath probably has one of the broadest and best-supported selections of CP/M software available. All these products are produced by companies that deal with the commercial marketplace and have produced office machines and computers for many years. Traditional office products manufacturers, such as Monroe, also have introduced well-structured systems. The primary advantage of these systems is that they, for the most part, conform to a large organization's demands and needs. Most of these companies have produced Z80-based systems, and several are working on 8086 or 8088 systems for the 16-bit market.

The S-100 Micros.   The earliest microcomputers produced during the mid-1970s were structured on a hardware configuration later dubbed the S-100 bus (a "bus" is simply the way in which electrical paths are organized). A large number of micros are still produced using this organization. It has the decided advantage over all others of being modular and capable of being configured to meet specific needs. Principal manufacturers include Vector Graphic, North Star, and Cromemco. These systems, manufactured

===

Listing 1
A Generalized Menu Program

```
100 '              A Generalized Menu Program
110 '                 by Thomas Wm. Madron
120 '
130 ' PURPOSE  -  To  provide  a  generalized  menu  program   for
140 '     executing  any program type (BASIC, /CMD, DO files, etc.)
150 '     under TRSDOS on a TRS-80  Model  III  microcomputer.    A
160 '     somewhat  different  approach would have to be taken with
170 '     CP/M based systems.  If, however, all programs were to be
180 '     in BASIC, then the present  system  would  run  with  few
190 '     modifications   under   any  version  of  Microsoft  BASIC
200 '     regardless of the Operating System used on the  computer.
210 '
220 ' Subroutines Used:
230 '
240 '     Bottom of Page Routine - Line 2000
250 '     Collect Character Stringe - Line 3000
260 '     Top of Screen Header Subroutine - Line 4000
270 '
280 ' Notes -
290 '
300 '      The  correct  filenames  are  acquired through  a  read of
310 ' the data statements.  Each data statement contains two items
320 ' of  information:  a filename and an English descriptor which
330 ' is printed on the screen as part of the menu.  The last data
340 ' statement must be the character string, "/*".   The  program
350 ' automatically  determines  the  number  of lines for the menu
360 ' and the menu can be more than one  screen  in  length.    In
370 ' fact, the menu can be any length at all.
380 '
390 CLEAR 2000
400 CLS
410 DEFINT A-Z
420 DEF FN CE$(A$, N)=STRING$(FIX((N-LEN(A$))/2)," ")+A$
430 DIM MN$(50), PG$(50)
440 NE=0
450 F1$="(##) %" +STRING$(50," ")+"%"
460 GOSUB 4160 ' Print Screen Header
470 '
480 ' Read MENU options from DATA statements
490 '
500 READ PG$(NE), MN$(NE)
510 IF PG$(NE)<>"/*" THEN NE=NE+1
    : GOTO 500
520 '
530 ' Print MENU
540 '
550 PRINT "SELECT FUNCTION BY NUMBER:"
560 PRINT
570 N1=10
580 FOR I=0 TO NE-1
590 IF I=N1 THEN GOSUB 2120 : N1=N1+10 ELSE 650
```

==

```
600 ON XX GOTO 610 , 610 , 720
610 CLS
620 PRINT "SELECT FUNCTION BY NUMBER:"
630 PRINT
640 GOTO 720
650 PRINT TAB(5); USING F1$; I+1; MN$(I)
660 NEXT I
670 IF I<=N1-1 OR I>N1-1 THEN GOSUB 2120
    : IF XX=1 THEN RUN
680 '
690 ' Determine appropriate choice and execute
700 '
710 ON ERROR GOTO 910
720 CLS
730 IF Y$=CHR$(13) OR Y<0 OR LEN(Y$)=0 THEN RUN
740 GOTO 790
750 ON ERROR GOTO 0
760 GOSUB 2120 ' Bottom of Page Routine
770 IF XX=1 THEN RUN
780 GOTO 720
790 IF INSTR(PG$(Y),"BASIC") THEN 870
800 IF INSTR(PG$(Y),"TRSDOS") THEN POKE 16916, 0
    : CLS
    : CMD "S"
810 IF INSTR(PG$(Y),"CMD") OR INSTR(PG$(Y),"BLD") THEN 820 ELSE 830
820 POKE 16916, 0
    : CLS
    : CMD "I",PG$(Y)
830 POKE 16916,0
    : CLS
    : RUN PG$(Y)
840 '
850 ' Remove Scroll Protect
860 '
870 POKE 16916, 0
880 CLS
890 END
900 '
910 ' Error Trapping Routine
920 '
930 IF ERR=106 THEN CLS
    : PRINT "File ";PG$(Y);" not found" ELSE 950
940 GOTO 990
950 CLS
960 PRINT "Unknown Error, Check TRSDOS Manual"
970 POKE 16916, 0
980 END
990 RESUME 750
1000 '
2000 '                         Bottom of Page Routine
2010 '
2020 ' PURPOSE - To terminate each page of the menu and  allow  for
2030 '      input of choice.
2040 '
2050 ' Notes -
```

===

```
2060 '
2070 '          When a page of the menu has been printed on the  screen
2080 ' the  user  may  then choose one of the options listed on the
2090 ' screen, press <ENTER> or press <R>.  If  the  menu  is  more
2100 ' than  one  screen  long,  then <ENTER> will display the next
2110 ' screen, otherwise it will have the same effect as <R>, which
2120 ' is to rerun the menu program itself.
2130 '
2140 PRINT
2150 PRINT @ 960,"WHICH FUNCTION (<ENTER> TO CONTINUE, 'R' TO RERUN)? ";
2160 GOSUB 3050 ' GET CHARACTER STRING
2170 IF Y$=CHR$(13) THEN XX=2: RETURN
2180 IF Y$="R" THEN RUN
2190 Y=VAL(Y$)-1
2200 IF Y>NE-1 THEN XX=1
   : RETURN
2210 XX=3
2220 RETURN
2230 '
3000 '                    Collect Character String
3010 '
3020 ' PURPOSE - To provide keyboard input for menu selection.  See
3030 '     note for "Bottom of Page Routine".
3040 '
3050 X$=""
3060 Z$=INKEY$
3070 IF Z$="" THEN 3060
3080 IF Z$=CHR$(8) THEN IF LEN(X$)>0 THEN X$=LEFT$(X$, LEN(X$)-1)
   : PRINT Z$;
   : GOTO 3060
3090 X$=X$+Z$
3100 IF Z$<>CHR$(13) THEN PRINT Z$; ELSE 3120
3110 GOTO 3060
3120 Y$=X$
3130 IF LEN(Y$)>1 THEN Y$=LEFT$(Y$, LEN(Y$)-1)
3140 RETURN
3150 '
4000 '                    Top of Screen Header
4010 '
4020 ' PURPOSE - To provide a neat heading for each  screen.    The
4030 '     screen  will have the word "MENU" centered, followed by a
4040 '     solid line (CHR$(131)) which is a graphics  character  on
4050 '     the  Model  III.    Other computers will have appropriate
4060 '     graphics or a character such as a minus sign or an  equal
4070 '     sign might be substituted.
4080 '
4090 ' Notes -
4100 '
4110 '          FNCE$ is a string centering  function  defined  at  the
4120 ' beginning  of  the  program.    Standard Microsoft BASIC
4130 ' possesses the DEF FN (define function) attribute.   If  such
4140 ' an  ability  is  not  present,  the  same  function could be
4150 ' rewritten as a standard subroutine.
4160 CLS
4170 PRINT FN CE$("MENU",64)+CHR$(10)+STRING$(64, 131);
```

73

==

```
4180 POKE 16916, 2
4190 RETURN
4200 '
5000 '                    DATA Statements
5010 '
5020 ' PURPOSE - To provide the  character  strings  necessary  for
5030 '     invoking particular programs or procedures and to provide
5040 '     the English text for the menu.
5050 '
5060 ' Notes -
5070 '
5080 '     The last DATA statement must contain the /* as well  as
5090 ' a null string ("").
5100 '
5110 DATA "NS/CMD","NEWSCRIPT Word Processor"
5120 DATA "VC/CMD","VISICALC Spreadsheet Program"
5130 DATA "PROFILE/CMD","PROFILE Data Management System"
5140 DATA "ST80III/CMD","ST80III Terminal Program"
5150 DATA "NOTEBOOK/BAS","NOTEBOOK (scratchpad) Program"
5160 DATA "APPT/BAS","APPOINTMENT Calendar"
5170 DATA "DSKMGT/BAS","Disk Management Menu"
5180 DATA "CHRSET/BAS","PRINTER Initialization"
5190 DATA "BASIC","EXIT to BASIC"
5200 DATA "TRSDOS","EXIT to TRSDOS"
5210 DATA "/*",""
```

AN APPOINTMENTS CALENDAR PROGRAM   DATE- TIME-
==

Listing 2
An Appointments Calendar Program

```
100 '          An Appointments Calendar Program
110 '                 by Thomas Wm. Madron
120 '
130 ' Limited  portions  of  this  program  as  well  as   several
140 '     organizational  ideas  were obtained from David D. Busch,
150 '     "By Appointment Only,"  80-MICROCOMPUTING,  March,  1981,
160 '     pp.  152-153.  Appropriate sections and concepts used by
170 '     permission of 80-MICROCOMPUTING.
180 '
190 '     Time management is a constant problem with any manager.
200 ' The behavior involved in keeping an appropriate calendar  is
210 ' neither trivial nor unimportant.  Although this program does
220 ' not  provide for all possible time management contingencies,
230 ' it does do well in maintaining a one  year  calendar.   The
240 ' program  dynamically  builds  a direct access file which, if
250 ' all days of the year are used, will have  a  length of  365
260 ' records  (256  bytes long) or 366 records in leap years.  It
270 ' is limited in that all entries for a single day cannot
280 ' exceed  a total of 255 characters or bytes.  This means that
290 ' it is possible to get more entries on a single day  if  each
300 ' entry is kept short.
310 '
```

```
320 '          When the program is first run it looks  (automatically)
330 ' for  an  appropriate  dataset,  named APPTSXX/CAL where "XX"
340 ' represents the last two digits of the current year (97,  for
350 ' example,  for  1997).  If an appropriate dataset is found, it
360 ' reads  the  record  for  the  current  date  and  prints  the
370 ' calendar  for  the  day.   Since the program uses the TRSDOS
380 ' system calendar it is important to set  the  date  correctly
390 ' when  the system is first turned on.  If an appropriate file
400 ' is not found,  a message and a short menu will  be  displayed
410 ' requesting  appropriate actions (place correct diskette in a
420 ' drive or return to the main menu).  If a new file is  to  be
430 ' created,  this may be done by simply typing one of the three
440 ' main commands (READ, WRITE, DELETE) followed  by  the  year
450 ' (full  four digits) for which the calendar is to be created.
460 ' More detail can be found in the HELP file, below.
470 '
480 ' Subroutines Used -
490 '
500 '      Take off Empty Spaces - Line 2000
510 '      Open Appointment File - Line 3000
520 '      Read Appointments - Line 4000
530 '      Convert Gregorian to Julian Dates - Line 5000
540 '      Convert Julian to Gregorian Dates - Line 6000
550 '      Get Date - Line 7000
560 '      Add (Write) Appointments - Line 8000
570 '      Get Calendar Year - Line 10000
580 '      Delete Calendar Entry - Line 11000
590 '      Get a Record - Line 12000
600 '      Put a Record - Line 13000
```

AN APPOINTMENTS CALENDAR PROGRAM   DATE- TIME-
==

```
610 '      Help File - Line 14000
620 '      Print Header - Line 16000
630 '      Wait for Input - Line 17000
640 '      Variable List Decoder - Line 18000
650 '      Disk File Error Routine - Line 19000
660 '      Demonstrate Current Date - Line 20000
670 '
680 ' Notes -
690 '
700 '          This program represents a major upgrade of the original
710 ' program cited above.  Although it is not necessary to make a
720 ' comparative list, suffice it to say that the current program
730 ' uses the disk file in a  substantially  different  manner,
740 ' deletions  are  more  global  in  nature,  the  help file is
750 ' available,  and  READ command is  more  flexible.   Other
760 ' improvements  could,  of  course,  be  made,  depending  on
770 ' immediate and long-term needs.
780 '
790 CLEAR 5000
800 DEFINT D, I-N
810 DIM APP$, DA$(20), LV(15)
820 '
830 ' DEF FNCE$(A$,N) defines a string centering function.  The
840 '      string (A$) is centered in a line N characters long.
850 '
```

```
860 DEF FN CE$(A$, N)=STRING$(FIX((N-LEN(A$))/2)," ")+A$
870 CLS ' CLS clears the screen on the TRS-80
880 PRINT FN CE$("APPOINTMENTS CALENDAR",64)
890 PRINT STRING$(64, 131); ' Prints a line of graphics characters
900 '
910 ' POKE 16916,2 Scroll protects the first two lines of the
920 '        display.  POKE 16916,0 removes the protection.
930 '
940 POKE 16916, 2
950 FOR I=0 TO 4
960 READ FL$(I)
970 NEXT I
980 DATA"READ","WRITE","DELETE","HELP","EXIT"
990 RESTORE
1000 NX=0
1010 KN=0
1020 GOSUB 20040   ' DISPLAY CURRENT DATE SCHEDULE
1030 GOTO 1060
1040 ID=2
1050 GOSUB 16100
1060 CLS
1070 PRINT"SELECT APPOINTMENT FUNCTION BY NAME:"
1080 PRINT
1090 PRINT"    READ <YEAR> - READ CURRENT APPOINTMENTS"
1100 PRINT"    WRITE <YEAR> - WRITE NEW APPOINTMENTS"
1110 PRINT"    DELETE <YEAR> - DELETE APPOINTMENT FROM FILE"
1120 PRINT"    HELP <FUNCTION> - APPOINTMENT CALENDAR INSTRUCTIONS"
1130 PRINT"    EXIT - EXIT TO SYSTEM"
1140 PRINT
1150 INPUT"WHICH FUNCTION";FU$


AN APPOINTMENTS CALENDAR PROGRAM                     DATE- TIME-
================================================================
1160 IF INSTR(FU$,"HELP")THEN GOSUB 14200
     : GOTO 1060
1170 IF INSTR(FU$,"EXIT") THEN 1350
1180 FOR I=0 TO 2
1190 IF INSTR(FU$, FL$(I)) THEN 1230
1200 NEXT I
1210 PRINT FU$;" IS AN INVALID FUNCTION NAME."
1220 GOTO 1140
1230 II=I+1
1240 JJ=LEN(FL$(I)): IF LEN(FU$)>JJ THEN YY$=RIGHT$(FU$,LEN(FU$)-JJ)
     : KN=0
1250 IF LEN(YY$) THEN GOSUB 2050 ELSE YY$=MID$(FU$, JJ+1)
     : GOSUB 2050
1260 IF KN=0 AND LEN(YY$) GOSUB 10050
     : GOSUB 3130
1270 KN=KN+1
1280 ON II GOTO 1290 , 1310 , 1330 , 1040  , 1350
1290 GOSUB 4180 ' READ APPOINTMENTS
1300 GOTO 1040
1310 GOSUB 8220 ' ADD APPOINTMENTS
1320 GOTO 1040
1330 GOSUB 11200 ' DELETE ENTRY FROM FILE
```

```
1340 GOTO 1040
1350 POKE 16916, 0
1360 CLOSE 1
1370 CLS
1380 RUN "MENU/BAS"
1390 '
2000 '              Subroutine - Take off Left Spaces
2010 '
2020 ' Purpose - To remove spaces at the  beginning  of  a  string.
2030 '    Used to edit strings containing <YEAR>.
2040 '
2050 IF LEFT$(YY$, 1)=" " THEN YY$=MID$(YY$, 2)
   : GOTO 2050
2060 RETURN
2070 '
3000 '              Subroutine - Open Appointment File
3010 '
3020 ' Purpose - Generalized routine to open the Calendar File  for
3030 '    an appropriate year.
3040 '
3050 ' Subroutines Used -
3060 '
3070 '    Get Calendar Year
3080 '    Disk File Error Routine (test for file) .
3090 '
3100 GOSUB 10050 ' CHECK CALENDAR YEAR AND COMPOSE Z$ (FILESPECS)
3110 GOSUB 19060  ' TEST FOR EXISTENCE OF FILE
3120 CLOSE 1
   : IF M1 THEN RETURN
3130 CLOSE 1
   : OPEN"R",1, Z$
3140 FIELD 1, 255ASXZ$
3150 CLS
```

```
3160 NX=1
3170 RETURN
3180 '
4000 '              Subroutine - Read Appointments
4010 '
4020 ' Purpose - A generalized input  routine  which  performs  the
4030 '    four  types  of  inquiries--Appointments  for  today,
4040 '    appointments for a specific day, appointments for a range
4050 '    of days, or appointments ranging from today  for  some
4060 '    specified number of days.
4070 '
4080 ' Subroutines Used -
4090 '
4100 '    Demo Current Date
4110 '    Convert Gregorian to Julian Dates
4120 '    Print Header
4130 '    Get a Record
4140 '    Wait for Input
4150 '    Convert Julian to Gregorian Dates
```

```
4160 '     Get Current Date
4170 '
4180 CLS
4190 PRINT"SELECT APPOINTMENTS (BY NUMBER):"
4200 PRINT
4210 PRINT TAB(5);"(1) FOR TODAY"
4220 PRINT TAB(5);"(2) FOR A SPECIFIC DAY"
4230 PRINT TAB(5);"(3) FOR A RANGE OF DAYS"
4240 PRINT TAB(5);"(4) DATE TO ? ... APPOINTMENT"
4250 PRINT TAB(5);"(5) RETURN TO MAIN MENU"
4260 PRINT
4270 PRINT"WHICH APPOINTMENT SET? ";
4280 Y$=INKEY$
4290 IF Y$="" THEN 4280
4300 IF VAL(Y$)<1 OR VAL(Y$)>5 THEN PRINT Y$
   : GOTO 4270
4310 PRINT Y$
4320 ON VAL(Y$) GOTO 4340 , 4420 , 4520 , 4770 , 4330
4330 RETURN
4340 '
4350 ' APPOINTMENTS FOR TODAY
4360 '
4370 GOSUB 20040 ' DEMO CURRENT DATE
4380 RETURN
4390 '
4400 '     APPOINTMENTS FOR A SPECIFIC DAY
4410 '
4420 GOSUB 5150 ' CONVERT DATE TO JULIAN
4430 GOSUB 16100  ' PRINT HEADING INCLUDING DATE SELECTED
4440 CLS
4450 GOSUB 12070   ' GET A RECORD
4460 PRINT APP$
4470 GOSUB 17060   ' WAIT FOR INPUT
4480 RETURN
4490 '
4500 '     APPOINTMENTS FOR A RANGE OF DAYS
```

```
4510 '
4520 CLS
4530 PRINT"ENTER LOWER DATE BOUNDARY"
4540 GOSUB 5160 ' CONVERT MM/DD TO JULIAN
4550 D1=DA
4560 PRINT"ENTER UPPER DATE BOUNDARY"
4570 GOSUB 5160 ' CONVERT MM/DD TO JULIAN
4580 D2=DA
4590 IF D2<D1 THEN 4600 ELSE 4610
4600 PRINT "UPPER DATE MUST BE GREATER THEN LOWER DATE": GOTO 4520
4610 CLS
4620 N=0
4630 FOR DA=D1 TO D2
4640 GOSUB 12070   ' GET A RECORD
4650 IF APP$="" THEN 4720
4660 DE$=STR$(DA)
4670 GOSUB 6130 ' CONVERT JULIAN TO MM/DD
4680 DA$=LEFT$(DE$, 5)
```

```
4690 GOSUB 16100   ' PRINT HEADING INCLUDING SELECTED DATE
4700 PRINT APP$
4710 GOSUB 17060   ' WAIT FOR INPUT
4720 NEXT DA
4730 RETURN
4740 '
4750 '       APPOINTMENTS FROM PRESENT DATE TO ?...
4760 '
4770 CLS
4780 GOSUB 7110 ' GET CURRENT DATE
4790 GOSUB 5180 ' CONVERT MM/DD TO JULIAN
4800 INPUT"APPOINTMENTS FOR HOW MANY DAYS";D2
4810 SO$="12/31/" +YY$
4820 CMD"J",SO$, DE$
4830 DZ=VAL(RIGHT$(DE$, 3))
4840 D2=DA+D2
4850 D1=DA
4860 IF D2>DZ THEN D2=DZ
4870 CLS
4880 FOR DA=D1 TO D2
4890 GOSUB 12070   ' GET A RECORD
4900 IF APP$="" THEN 4970
4910 DE$=STR$(DA)
4920 GOSUB 6130 ' CONVERT JULIAN TO MM/DD
4930 DA$=LEFT$(DE$, 5)
4940 GOSUB 16100   ' PRINT HEADING INCLUDING SELECTED DATE
4950 PRINT APP$
4960 GOSUB 17060   ' WAIT FOR INPUT
4970 NEXT DA
4980 RETURN
4990 '
5000 '         Subroutine - Convert Gregorian to Julian Dates
5010 '
5020 ' Purpose - To convert Gregorian dates in the form MM/DD/YY to
5030 '     Julian Dates in the form DDD/YY.
5040 '
5050 ' Notes -
```

AN APPOINTMENTS CALENDAR PROGRAM   DATE- TIME-
==

```
5060 '
5070 '       The actual conversion of the  date  is  done  with  the
5080 ' system  subroutine, CMD "J",AA$,BB$.  Systems other than  the
5090 ' TRS-80 Model III may not have such  subroutines.     In  that
5100 ' event  it  would  be  necessary  to  provide  an  appropriate
5110 ' routine in BASIC. One source for such a subroutine is  John
5120 ' P.  Bauernschub,  Jr.,  "The  BASIC  Dating  Game," KILOBAUD
5130 ' MICROCOMPUTING, May 1980, pp. 208-212.
5140 '
5150 CLS
5160 DA=0
5170 INPUT"ENTER DATE (MM/DD): ";DA$
5180 IF LEN(DA$)=5 AND INSTR(DA$,"/")THEN 5210
5190 PRINT"THE DATE MUST BE ENTERED IN THE FORMAT 'MM/DD'"
5200 GOTO 5170
5210 M$=LEFT$(DA$, 2)
5220 D$=RIGHT$(DA$, 2)
```

```
5230 M=VAL(M$)
5240 D=VAL(D$)
5250 SO$=DA$+"/" +YY$
5260 CMD"J",SO$, DE$
5270 DA=VAL(RIGHT$(DE$, 3))
5280 RETURN
5290 '
6000 '          Subroutine - Convert Julian to Gregorian
6010 '
6020 ' Purpose - To convert Julian dates  in  the  form  DDD/YY  to
6030 '     Gregorian dates in the form MM/DD/YY.
6040 '
6050 ' Notes -
6060 '
6070 '     This  routine,  like  its  reverse,  uses  the  system
6080 ' subroutine CMD "J",AA$,BB$ to do the actual conversion.  For
6090 ' other  systems an appropriate BASIC routine would have to be
6100 ' substituted. See the reference for  "Convert  Gregorian  to
6110 ' Julian".
6120 '
6130 IF LEFT$(DE$,1)=" " THEN DE$=MID$(DE$,2)
     : GOTO 6130
6140 DE$=STRING$(3-LEN(DE$),"0")+DE$
6150 SO$="-"+YY$+"/"+RIGHT$(DE$,3)
6160 CMD"J",SO$, DE$
6170 M=VAL(LEFT$(DE$, 2))
6180 F1=VAL(MID$(DE$, 4, 2))
6190 RETURN
6200 '
7000 '               Subroutine - Get Date
7010 '
7020 ' Purpose - To obtain the current date from the system  clock.
7030 '     Other  systems  handle this problem differently than does
7040 '     the TRS-80 Model III which uses  the  function  TIME$  to
7050 '     provide  both the current time and date.  In many systems
7060 '     it  would  be  necessary  to PEEK  appropriate  storage
7070 '     locations    normally   documented   in    the   system
7080 '     documentation. Another alternative woul
```

AN APPOINTMENTS CALENDAR PROGRAM   DATE- TIME-
==

```
5060 '
5070 '     The actual conversion of  the  date  is  done  with  the
5080 ' system  subroutine, CMD "J",AA$,BB$.  Systems other than the
5090 ' TRS-80 Model III may not have such  subroutines.    In  that
5100 ' event  it  would  be  necessary  to  provide  an appropriate
5110 ' routine in BASIC.  One source for such a subroutine is  John
5120 ' P.  Bauernschub,  Jr.,  "The  BASIC  Dating  Game," KILOBAUD
5130 ' MICROCOMPUTING, May 1980, pp. 208-212.
5140 '
5150 CLS
5160 DA=0
5170 INPUT"ENTER DATE (MM/DD): ";DA$
5180 IF LEN(DA$)=5 AND INSTR(DA$,"/")THEN 5210
5190 PRINT"THE DATE MUST BE ENTERED IN THE FORMAT 'MM/DD'"
5200 GOTO 5170
```

```
5210 M$=LEFT$(DA$, 2)
5220 D$=RIGHT$(DA$, 2)
5230 M=VAL(M$)
5240 D=VAL(D$)
5250 SO$=DA$+"/" +YY$
5260 CMD"J",SOS, DE$
5270 DA=VAL(RIGHT$(DE$, 3))
5280 RETURN
5290 '
6000 '              Subroutine - Convert Julian to Gregorian
6010 '
6020 ' Purpose - To convert Julian dates  in  the  form  DDD/YY  to
6030 '     Gregorian dates in the form MM/DD/YY.
6040 '
6050 ' Notes -
6060 '
6070 '     This  routine,  like  its  reverse,  uses  the  system
6080 ' subroutine CMD "J",AA$,BB$ to do the actual conversion.  For
6090 ' other  systems  an appropriate BASIC routine would have to be
6100 ' substituted.  See the reference for  "Convert  Gregorian  to
6110 ' Julian".
6120 '
6130 IF LEFT$(DE$,1)=" " THEN DE$=MID$(DE$,2)
     : GOTO 6130
6140 DE$=STRING$(3-LEN(DE$),"0")+DE$
6150 SO$="-"+YY$+"/"+RIGHT$(DE$,3)
6160 CMD"J",SOS, DE$
6170 M=VAL(LEFT$(DE$, 2))
6180 F1=VAL(MID$(DE$, 4, 2))
6190 RETURN
6200 '
7000 '                  Subroutine - Get Date
7010 '
7020 ' Purpose - To obtain the current date from the system  clock.
7030 '     Other  systems  handle this problem differently than does
7040 '     the TRS-80 Model III which uses  the  function  TIME$  to
7050 '     provide  both the current time and date.  In many systems
7060 '     it  would  be  necessary  to  PEEK  appropriate  storage
7070 '     locations  normally  documented  in  the  system
7080 '     documentation.  Another alternative would be to provide a
```

==

```
7090 '     specific input routine for keyboard input.
7100 '
7110 DA$=LEFT$(TIME$, 5)
     : Y1$=MID$(TIME$,7,2)
7120 GOSUB 5210 ' CONVERT MM/DD TO JULIAN
7130 RETURN
7140 '
8000 '                  Subroutine - Write Appointments
8010 '
8020 ' Purpose - To Write new appointments to the file.
8030 '
8040 ' Subroutines Used -
8050 '
```

```
8060 '    Get a Record
8070 '    Put a Record
8080 '
8090 ' Notes -
8100 '
8110 '    During the process of constructing the string
8120 ' containing the appointment record, the entries for a
8130 ' particular day are sorted by time into ascending order. The
8140 ' system subroutine CMD "O" is used for the sort.    On the
8150 ' Model III disk system CMD "O" will sort a string array into
8160 ' ascending order. On other systems a sort subroutine in
8170 ' BASIC or Assembler would have to be provided. One source
8180 ' for a sort routine is Dennie Van Tassel, BASIC-PACK
8190 ' STATISTICS PROGRAMS FOR SMALL COMPUTERS (Englewood Cliffs,
8200 ' NJ: Prentice-Hall, Inc., 1981), pp. 72-76 (see program
8210 ' lines 1500 to 1580 for a simple bubble sort).
8220 '
8230 ' Housekeeping
8240 '
8250 '    APP$ = Variable used for GETting and PUTting data
8260 '             to the calendar for each day.
8270 '
8280 '    A$ = Variable used for constructing current entry.
8290 '
8300 ' The following section requests entry of the DATE, TIME,
8310 ' and nature of the appointment.  The program then con-
8320 ' structs, using A$, a properly formatted string.
8330 '
8340 APP$=""
8350 A$=""
8360 '
8370 ' IF NX<>0 THEN CONVERT MM/DD TO JULIAN, OTHERWISE
8380 '     OPEN CALENDAR FILE THEN CONVERT MM/DD TO JULIAN
8390 '
8400 IF NX THEN GOSUB 5150 ELSE GOSUB 3100
   : GOSUB 5150
8410 IF M1 THEN CLOSE 1
   : GOSUB 3130
8420 PRINT"ENTER APPOINTMENT:"
8430 LINE INPUT"TIME (HH:MM) OF APPOINTMENT: ";TM$
8440 IF INSTR(TM$,":")AND LEN(TM$)=5 THEN 8470
8450 PRINT"TIME MUST BE IN THE FORMAT 'HH:MM'"
```

```
8460 GOTO 8430
8470 INPUT"(A)M OR (P)M";PM$
8480 IF LEFT$(PM$, 1)="A" THEN PM$="A.M." ELSE PM$="P.M."
8490 LINE INPUT"WITH WHOM? ";A$
8500 A$=TM$+" " +PM$+" - " +A$
8510 '
8520 ' The disk file is accessed to check for existing entries
8530 ' for the same date.
8540 '
8550 GOSUB 12070   ' GET A RECORD
8560 '
```

```
8570 ' When the record is obtained, it is then checked to see
8580 ' whether or not it is blank.
8590 '
8600 IF APP$=STRING$(255,0) OR APP$=STRING$(255,32) THEN APP$=""
8610 FOR I=255 TO 2 STEP -1
8620 IF RIGHT$(APP$,1)=" " THEN APP$=LEFT$(APP$,I-1)
8630 NEXT I
8640 '
8650 ' The current entry is then appended to previous entries
8660 ' if such entries exist.
8670 '
8680 APP$=APP$+A$+CHR$(10)
8690 '
8700 ' The data contained in APP$ are segmented with each
8710 ' complete appointment placed in DA(i) and the time of
8720 ' each appointment placed in IN$(i).  IN$(i) is then
8730 ' sorted and is used as an index to reconstruct APP$.
8740 '
8750 II=1
8760 NN=0
8770 JJ=INSTR(II, APP$, CHR$(10))
8780 IF JJ THEN 8790 ELSE 8820
8790 DA$(NN)=MID$(APP$,II,JJ-II+1)
8800 IN$(NN)=LEFT$(DA$(NN),12)+RIGHT$(STR$(NN),2)
8810 II=JJ+1: NN=NN+1: GOTO 8770
8820 FOR I=0 TO NN-1
8830 II=INSTR(IN$(I),":")
8840 IF INSTR(IN$(I),"P")THEN JJ=VAL(IN$(I))+12 ELSE 8860
8850 IN$(I)=RIGHT$(STR$(JJ), 2)+MID$(IN$(I), II)
8860 NEXT I
8870 CMD"O",NN, IN$(0)
8880 '
8890 ' Reconstruct APP$ in sorted order.
8900 '
8910 APP$=""
8920 NN=NN-1
3930 FOR I=0 TO NN
8940 LL=VAL(RIGHT$(IN$(I), 2))
8950 KK=VAL(IN$(I))
8960 IF KK>12 THEN MID$(DA$(LL), 1, 2)=RIGHT$(STR$(KK-12), 2)
8970 IF KK>12 AND KK<22 THEN DA$(LL)="0" +MID$(DA$(LL), 2)
8980 APP$=APP$+DA$(LL)
8990 NEXT I
9000 '
```

```
9010 ' Rewrite APP$ to disk file
9020 '
9030 GOSUB 13070   ' PUT A RECORD
9040 RETURN
9050 '
10000 '                Subroutine - Get Calendar Year
10010 '
10020 ' Purpose - To obtain calendar year from keyboard
10030 '
```

```
10040 LINE INPUT"ENTER CALENDAR YEAR (YYYY): ";YY$
10050 IF LEN(YY$)<>4 THEN PRINT"YEAR MUST HAVE FOUR DIGITS": GOTO 10040
10060 YY$=RIGHT$(YY$, 2)
10070 Z$="APPTS" +YY$+"/CAL"
10080 RETURN
10090 '
11000 '                    Subroutine - Delete Calendar Entry
11010 '
11020 ' Purpose - To allow the deletion of  one  or  more  calendar
11030 '     entries for a particular date.
11040 '
11050 ' Subroutines Used -
11060 '
11070 '     Variable List Decoder
11080 '     Convert Gregorian to Julian
11090 '     Get a Record
11100 '     Put a Record
11110 '
11120 ' Notes -
11130 '
11140 '     When executed this  subroutine  presents  each  of  the
11150 ' entries  for  a day, numbering each one as a menu item.   The
11160 ' user may then delete one or more entries  by  number  or  an
11170 ' explicit  series  (1,2,3,...,n)  of  numbers  or an  implicit
11180 ' series (1-n, where '-' means nl 'through' n2).
11190 '
11200 CLS
11210 PRINT"DELETE CALENDAR ENTRY"
11220 GOSUB 5160 ' CONVERT MM/DD TO JULIAN
11230 GOSUB 12070   ' GET A RECORD
11240 II=1
11250 NN=0
11260 JJ=INSTR(II, APP$, CHR$(10))
11270 IF JJ THEN DA$(NN)=MID$(APP$, II, JJ-II)
    : II=JJ+1
    : NN=NN+1
    : GOTO 11260
11280 CLS
11290 NN=NN-1
11300 F1$="## %" +STRING$(58, 32)+"%"
11310 FOR I=0 TO NN
11320 II=LEN(DA$(I))
11330 IF II>60 THEN II=60
11340 PRINT USING F1$; I+1; LEFT$(DA$(I), II)
11350 NEXT I
11360 PRINT
```

```
11370 PRINT"DELETE ENTRIES BY NUMBER"
11380 GOSUB 18350 ' VARIABLE LIST DECODER
11390 IF NV=0 THEN RETURN
11400 APP$=""
11410 IF NV-1=NN THEN 11470
11420 FOR I=0 TO NN
11430 FOR J=0 TO NV-1
```

```
11440 IF I+1=LV(J)THEN 11460
    : NEXT J
11450 APP$=APP$+DA$(I)+CHR$(10)
11460 NEXT I
11470 GOSUB 13070  ' PUT A RECORD
11480 RETURN
11490 '
12000 '                  Subroutine - Get a Record
12010 '
12020 ' Purpose - To get a direct access record .(APP$) for a
12030 '     particular day (DA).
12040 '
12050 ' APP$ = APPOINTMENTS FOR A DAY; DA=DATE (JULIAN)
12060 '
12070 APP$=""
12080 GET 1, DA
12090 APP$=XZ$
12100 RETURN
12110 '
13000 '                  Subroutine - Put a Record
13010 '
13020 ' Purpose - To put a direct access record (APP$) for a
13030 '     particular day (DA).
13040 '
13050 ' APP$=APPOINTMENTS FOR A DAY; DA=DATE (JULIAN)
13060 '
13070 LSET XZ$=APP$
13080 PUT 1, DA
13090 RETURN
13100 '
14000 '                  Subroutine - Help File
14010 '
14020 ' Purpose - To provide help for each function  or  command  in
14030 '     the calendar program.
14040 '
14050 ' Subroutines Used -
14060 '
14070 '     Display Prompt
14080 '     Test Response (to prompt)
14090 '
14100 ' Notes -
14110 '
14120 '      Each Help file consists of a number of formatted  print
14130 ' statements  designed  for  the  64 x 16 screen of the TRS-80
14140 ' Model III.  After each help file is printed  a  flashing
14150 ' prompt  (<---,X,--->)  is printed indicating which arrows to
14160 ' press for the previous help message, eXit to the main  menu,
14170 ' or  move to the next help message.  The two subroutines used
```

```
14180 ' display the prompt and decipher the response to the  prompt.
14190 '
14200 POKE 16916,0
    : CLS
    : II=INSTR(FU$,"HELP")+4
    : HE$=MID$(FU$,II)
```

```
14210 IF LEN(HE$)<4 THEN 14270
14220 FOR I=0 TO 4
14230 IF INSTR(HE$,FL$(I)) THEN J=I+1
    : I=0
    : GOTO 14250
14240 NEXT I
14250 ON J GOTO 14450 ,14610 ,14740 ,14270 ,14910
14260 RETURN
14270 CLS
    : PRINT"                    HELP <FUNCTION>"
14280 PRINT" "
14290 PRINT"     The help file is designed to assist  the  user  of  the"
14300 PRINT"Appointments  Calendar  Program  to   use   the   software"
14310 PRINT"effectively. With all commands, elements enclosed  in  less"
14320 PRINT"than  (<)  and greater than (>) symbols are optional. There"
14330 PRINT"are five commands:  READ, WRITE,  DELETE,  HELP,  and  EXIT."
14340 PRINT"Each does exactly the task implied for a calendar entry.  If"
14350 PRINT"an  appropriate file does not exist for a given year, it may"
14360 PRINT"be created by simply typing one  of  the  dynamic  commands,"
14370 PRINT"READ, WRITE, or DELETE, followed by a space and the complete"
14380 PRINT"four digit year.  Other help files can be accessed from this"
14390 PRINT"point by pressing the left arrow (<--) for the previous help"
14400 PRINT"file,  the  right arrow (-->) for the next help file, or 'X'"
14410 PRINT"to return to the main menu.  "
14420 GOSUB 15030 ' DISPLAY PROMPT
14430 GOSUB 15100 ' TEST RESPONSE
14440 ON J GOTO 14450 ,14610 ,14740 ,14270 ,14910 ,15020
14450 CLS
    : PRINT"                    READ <YEAR>"
14460 PRINT" "
14470 PRINT"     The READ command allows the user to read  one  or  more"
14480 PRINT"records for a given <YEAR>.  If the file for the appropriate"
14490 PRINT"year  already  exists,  then  YEAR is optional. If the user"
14500 PRINT"wishes to create a new calendar or to read a calendar  other"
14510 PRINT"than that for the current year, then YEAR is required.  When"
14520 PRINT"READ is typed, a new menu will appear.  The user may then"
14530 PRINT"select today's record, the record for  some  other  specific"
14540 PRINT"day, records for an arbitrary range of days, or records from"
14550 PRINT"today's  date  to some arbitrary point in the future.  These"
14560 PRINT"features allow the user to  review  an  entire  week,  or  a"
14570 PRINT"month, for that matter.  "
14580 GOSUB 15030 ' DISPLAY PROMPT
14590 GOSUB 15100 ' TEST RESPONSE
14600 ON J GOTO 14450 ,14610 ,14740 ,14270 ,14910 ,15020
14610 CLS
    : PRINT"                    WRITE <YEAR>"
14620 PRINT" "
14630 PRINT"     WRITE allows the user to add new  appointments  to  the"
14640 PRINT"calendar.  Like the commands READ and DELETE, WRITE can also"
```

AN APPOINTMENTS CALENDAR PROGRAM   DATE- TIME-
===

```
14650 PRINT"be  used  to open a new file for a new year by appending the"
14660 PRINT"year to the command.  If more than one calendar is available"
14670 PRINT"on disk (last year or next  year,  for  example),  appending"
14680 PRINT"<YEAR>  will  also  allow  the user to move from the current"
14690 PRINT"year's calendar to the year designated.  Dates  must  always"
```

```
14700 PRINT"be  displayed in MM/DD format and times in the HH:MM format."
14710 GOSUB 15030 ' DISPLAY PROMPT
14720 GOSUB 15100 ' TEST RESPONSE
14730 ON J GOTO 14450 ,14610 ,14740 ,14270 ,14910 ,15020
14740 CLS
     : PRINT"                              DELETE <YEAR>"
14750 PRINT" "
14760 PRINT"       Delete allows the user to delete one  or  more  entries"
14770 PRINT"from  the  calendar  for  a  particular day.  The date is in"
14780 PRINT"MM/DD format.  When a date is entered following issuing  the"
14790 PRINT"'DELETE'  command the calendar for the day is presented as a"
14800 PRINT"numbered menu.  The program then waits for input.  Input may"
14810 PRINT"be  one  or  more  numbers  designating  the  entries  to  be"
14820 PRINT"deleted.   If there are five entries, for example, they will"
14830 PRINT"be numbered in chronological order.  The user may then enter"
14840 PRINT"a string and/or range of numbers:  1,2,3,4 or 1-4.  A  range"
14850 PRINT"of  numbers  consists  of  the  first  entry  to be deleted,"
14860 PRINT"followed by a hyphen (-), followed by the last entry  to  be"
14870 PRINT"deleted.        "
14880 GOSUB 15030 ' DISPLAY PROMPT
14890 GOSUB 15100 ' TEST RESPONSE
14900 ON J GOTO 14450 ,14610 ,14740 ,14270 ,14910 ,15020
14910 CLS
     : PRINT"                              EXIT"
14920 PRINT" "
14930 PRINT"       Issuing  the  EXIT  command  will  close  the  current"
14940 PRINT"calendar  file and exit to the system menu (MENU/BAS).  This"
14950 PRINT"may be changed, of course, to exit to BASIC or to DOS.    In"
14960 PRINT"any event, when the user is finished using the calendar, the"
14970 PRINT"EXIT  command should always be used for an orderly exit from"
14980 PRINT"the program.     "
14990 GOSUB 15030 ' DISPLAY PROMPT
15000 GOSUB 15100 ' TEST RESPONSE
15010 ON J GOTO 14450 ,14610 ,14740 ,14270 ,14910 ,15020
15020 ID=2: POKE 16916,2: GOSUB 16100
     : RETURN
15030 ' FLASH PROMPT, GET CHARACTER
15040 PRINT @ 960,FNCE$("<---,X,--->",64);
15050 FOR XX=1 TO 100: NEXT XX
15060 PRINT @ 960,FNCE$(STRING$(11," "),64);
15070 FOR XX=1 TO 100: NEXT XX
15080 Y$=INKEY$
     : IF Y$="" THEN 15040
15090 CLS: RETURN
15100 ' TEST RESPONSE
15110 IF Y$=CHR$(8) THEN J=J-1
     : IF J<=0 THEN J=1
     : RETURN ELSE RETURN
15120 IF Y$=CHR$(88) THEN J=6
     : RETURN
```

```
15130 IF Y$=CHR$(9) THEN J=J+1
     : IF J>5 THEN J=5
     : RETURN ELSE RETURN
15140 RETURN
```

```
15150 '
16000 '          Subroutine - Print Header Including Current Date
16010 '
16020 ' Purpose - To print a header at the top of each screen.
16030 '
16040 ' Notes -
16050 '
16060 '      The statement, PRINT @ 0, ... , prints a line at line 0
16070 ' (first line) of the display.  Other systems will have to use
16080 ' other screen formatting techniques.
16090 '
16100 DT$="APPOINTMENTS CALENDAR"
16110 PRINT @ 0, CHR$(31);
16120 IF ID=2 THEN ID=0: GOTO 16140
16130 DT$="APPOINTMENTS CALENDAR FOR " +DA$+"/" +YY$
16140 PRINT @ 0, FN CE$(DT$, 64)
16150 PRINT STRING$(64, 131);
16160 CLS
16170 RETURN
16180 '
17000 '                  Subroutine - Wait for Input
17010 '
17020 ' Purpose - To print a message at the last line of the display
17030 '      (using PRINT @ 960,...), then wait for a  response  using
17040 '      the INKEY$ function.
17050 '
17060 PRINT @ 960, FN CE$("Press ANY key to continue",64);
17070 IF INKEY$ ="" THEN 17070
17080 RETURN
17090 '
18000 '          Subroutine - Variable List Decoder (2)
18010 '
18020 ' PURPOSE - To read a string from the keyboard composed of
18030 '      numbers, commas, and/or hyphens and to return  a
18040 '      vector containing the numbers stated or implied.
18050 '
18060 ' Important Variables:
18070 '
18080 '      NV:       Total number of values returned.
18090 '
18100 '      LV(I):  Array containing the vector of values read.
18110 '
18120 ' Notes:
18130 '
18140 '      This routine allows for the  input  of  a  string  of
18150 ' numbers on a single line without the need for specifying
18160 ' an  explicit  number  of  variables  (as  with the INPUT
18170 ' statement in BASIC).    When using  the  subroutine  to
18180 ' process  a  string of integers (returned in LV(I)), each
18190 ' of the following is acceptable:
18200 '
```

AN APPOINTMENTS CALENDAR PROGRAM   DATE- TIME-
==

```
18210 '    1,2,3,4,5
18220 '
18230 '    1-5
```

```
18240 '
18250 '      1-3,4,5
18260 '
18270 '      In each of the illustrations LV(I)  (locations  0-4)
18280 ' would return with the number l to 5 and NV would = 5.  A
18290 ' string  of  continuous  and  contiguous  number  can  be
18300 ' entered  using the beginning and ending number separated
18310 ' by a hyphen.  Thus,  1-5  means  a  string  of  numbers
18320 ' consisting  of  the  integers l to 5 inclusive of both l
18330 ' and 5.  A carriage return <ENTER> terminates the string.
18340 '
18350 V$="":Vl$="":K=0
    :Ll=0
    :L2=0
18360 PRINT "ENTER NUMBER LIST: ":LINEINPUT V$
18370 IF LEN(V$)=0 THEN RETURN
18380 ' SEARCH FOR INDIVIDUAL VARIABLES
18390 Ll=INSTR(V$,",")
18400 IF Ll>0 THEN Vl$=LEFT$(V$,Ll-1)
    : V$=MID$(V$,Ll+1)
18410 IF Ll=0 THEN Vl$=V$
    : V$=""
18420 L2=INSTR(Vl$,"-")
18430 IF L2 THEN 18460
18440 LV(K)=VAL(Vl$): K=K+1
    : NV=K
    : GOTO 18370
18450 ' BEGIN LOOP FOR CONTIGUOUS VARS
18460 V2=VAL(MID$(Vl$,1,3))
    : V3=VAL(MID$(Vl$,L2+1,3))
18470 FOR I=V2 TO V3
    :LV(K)=I
    :K=K+1
    :NEXT I
18480 NV=K
    :GOTO 18370
18490 '
19000 '              Subroutine - Disk File Error Routine
19010 '
19020 ' Purpose - To provide  an  error  handling  routine  designed
19030 '    primarily  for  the testing of the presence or absence of
19040 '    an appropriate calendar file.
19050 '
19060 Ml=0
19070 ON ERROR GOTO 19130
19080 CLOSE 1
19090 OPEN "I",1,Z$
19100 ON ERROR GOTO 0
19110 CLOSE 1
19120 RETURN
19130 Ml=ERR/2+1
19140 IF Ml=54 THEN CLS
```

AN APPOINTMENTS CALENDAR PROGRAM   DATE- TIME-
==

```
    : PRINT FNCE$("File "+Z$+" not found",64)
19150 PRINT
```

```
19160 PRINT"PLEASE TAKE ONE OF THE FOLLOWING ACTIONS: "
19170 PRINT
19180 PRINT TAB(5);"(1) PLACE CORRECT DISK IN DRIVE THEN PRESS (1)"
19190 PRINT TAB(5);"(2) PRESS (2) TO RETURN TO MENU"
19200 PRINT
19210 PRINT"WHICH ACTION? "
19220 Y$=INKEY$
19230 IF Y$="" THEN 19220
19240 IF Y$<"1" OR Y$>"2" THEN CLS
     : GOTO 19160
19250 ON VAL(Y$) GOTO 19260 , 19270
19260 CLOSE 1
     : RUN
19270 RETURN
19280 CLOSE 1
19290 RESUME 19080
19300 '
20000 '              Subroutine - Demo Current Date
20010 '
20020 ' Purpose - To print the calendar for the current date.
20030 '
20040 GOSUB 7110 ' GET CURRENT DATE
20050 IF KN THEN 20110
20060 YY$=Y1$
     : GOSUB 10070 ' CONSTRUCT FILESPEC
20070 GOSUB 19060  ' TEST PRESENCE OF FILESPEC
20080 IF M1=54 THEN RETURN
20090 GOSUB 3120 ' OPEN APPOINTMENT FILE
20100 GOSUB 5210 ' CONVERT TO JULIAN
20110 GOSUB 4430 ' PRINT CURRENT DATE CALENDAR
20120 IF KN=0 THEN ID=2
     : GOSUB 16100 ' PRINT HEADER
20130 KN=1
     : RETURN
```

A NOTEBOOK PROGRAM   DATE- TIME-
===

Listing 3
A NOTEBOOK PROGRAM

```
100 '                    A Notebook Program
110 '                    by Thomas Wm. Madron
120 '
130 ' This program was adapted from the  PERCOM  NOTEBOOK  program
140 '    [(c) Percom  Data  Company, Inc.] running under Percom's
150 '    OS-80 [Trademark of Percom Data Company, Inc.]  operating
160 '    system  for  the  TRS-80 Model III.  The program has been
170 '    changed extensively with additions  and  adaptations  for
180 '    TRSDOS,  Tandy's  operating system.  Appropriate segments
190 '    used by permission of Percom Data Company, Inc.
200 '
210 '        For any  manager  notetaking  is  a  constant  problem.
220 ' Especially  as  more  functions  of  a  manager's office are
230 ' computerized, it is desirable that a notetaking function  be
240 ' easily  and  quickly  available.  The purpose of this program,
250 ' therefore, is to provide a means for recording notes on  any
```

```
260 ' topic.  This program allows the user to define a notebook of
270 ' "n"  pages plus a table of contents page.  It is possible to
280 ' update the notebook by additions and deletions.   While  the
290 ' notebook  program contains its own primitive text editor, an
300 ' additional  function,  'GETFILE', allows the user to prepare
310 ' and format text with a word processor and then add that file
320 ' to the notebook.  Hence, the notebook program can provide  a
330 ' useful  method  for  maintaining  online  documentation  of
340 ' current projects.
350 '
360 ' Subroutines Used -
370 '
380 '     HELP Files function - Line 2000
390 '     READ function - Line 3000
400 '     WRITE function - Line 4000
410 '     NEW Function - Line 5000
420 '     BOTTOM-OF-PAGE routine - Line 6000
430 '     FLASH PROMPT--GET CHARACTER - Line 7000
440 '     GET PAGE NUMBER FROM FUNCTION LINE - Line 8000
450 '     Load Table of Contents - Line 9000
460 '     Write Table of Contents - Line 10000
470 '     GETFILE Function - Line 11000
480 '
490 ' Notes -
500 '
510 '     The  Notebook  system  uses  a   random   access   file
520 ' structure.  The total number of pages is established by the
530 ' NEW function which initializes the appropriate  disk  space.
540 ' The  HELP  files allow the user to obtain instruction on the
550 ' use of the system as it is being used.  Hence, the  Notebook
560 ' is self documenting.
570 '
580 ' Housekeeping and Initialization
590 '
600 CLEAR 5000
```

===

```
610 DEFINT A-Z
620 NP=5
630 DIM B$(3), LN$(15), PR$(NP)
640 DEF FN UL$(C$)=CHR$(ASC(C$)+32*(95<ASC(C$)))
650 DEF FNCE$(A$,N)=STRING$(FIX((N-LEN(A$))/2)," ")+A$+CHR$(10)+STRING$(64,131)
660 CLS
670 PRINT @ 0, FN CE$("NOTEBOOK",64);
680 FOR I=0 TO NP
690 READ PR$(I)
700 NEXT I
710 DATA READ, WRITE, GETFILE, NEW, HELP, EXIT
720 RESTORE
730 LINE INPUT "NOTEBOOK FILESPECS <FILENM/EXT:D#>: ";FI$
740 IF FI$="" THEN CLS
    : END
750 OPEN "R",1, FI$
760 FIELD 1, 255 AS BF$
770 I=INSTR(FI$,":")
```

```
780 IF I<>0 THEN DR=VAL(MID$(FI$, I+1)) ELSE DR=0
790 FS=1
800 DEF FN SC(PG)=PG*4    ' RETURNS SECTOR ADDRESS OF PAGE (PG)
810 LA$="<--"
820 RA$="-->"   ' CONSTANTS
830 DIM TC$(47), TC(47)   ' TABLE OF CONTENTS
840 '
850 ' Print NOTEBOOK Menu
860 '
870 CLS
880 MP=( LOF(1))/4'CALCULATE NUMBER OF PAGES
890 PRINT FN CE$("NOTEBOOK MENU",64);
900 PRINT "FUNCTIONS AVAILABLE:"
910 PRINT
920 PRINT "  READ <PAGE> - DISPLAY PAGE(S) OF THE NOTEBOOK"
930 PRINT "  WRITE <PAGE> - ENTER PAGE(S) OF DATA INTO THE NOTEBOOK"
940 PRINT "  GETFILE - GET A DISK FILE"
950 PRINT "  NEW - CREATE A NEW (COMPLETELY BLANK) NOTEBOOK"
960 PRINT "  HELP - MORE INFORMATION ABOUT THE NOTEBOOK"
970 PRINT "  EXIT - RETURN TO SYSTEM"
980 PRINT
990 FC$=""
1000 INPUT "FUNCTION";FC$
1010 IF FC$="" THEN 870
1020 CLS
1030 '
1040 ' Execute Selected Function
1050 '
1060 FOR I=0 TO NP
1070 IF INSTR(FC$, PR$(I)) THEN J=I+1
    : I=0
    : GOTO 1110
1080 NEXT I
1090 PRINT "*** ";FC$;" IS AN INVALID FUNCTION"
1100 GOTO 990
1110 ON J GOTO 1120, 1140, 1170, 1200, 1220, 1300
1120 GOSUB 3200 ' READ FUNCTION
```

```
1130 GOTO 870
1140 GT=0
1150 GOSUB 4250 ' WRITE FUNCTION
1160 GOTO 870
1170 GT=1
1180 GOSUB 4250 ' GETFILE FUNCTION
1190 GOTO 870
1200 GOSUB 5030 ' NEW FUNCTION
1210 GOTO 870
1220 GOSUB 2190 ' HELP FUNCTION
1230 GOTO 870
1240 '
1250 ' EXIT FUNCTION - Close file then runs the system menu.
1260 '      The EXIT function should ALWAYS be used to terminate
1270 '      NOTEBOOK so that the NOTEBOOK file can be properly
1280 '      closed.
```

```
1290 '
1300 CLOSE 1
1310 CLS
1320 RUN "MENU/BAS"
1330 '
2000 '                      Subroutine - Help Files
2010 '
2020 ' Purpose - To provide assistance and instruction for the  use
2030 '     of  NOTEBOOK/BAS.   Help is available for all functions.
2040 '     Consequently, the program is self  documenting  and  self
2050 '     instructional.
2060 '
2070 ' Subroutines Used -
2080 '
2090 '     Flash Prompt
2100 '
2110 ' Notes -
2120 '
2130 '      In the present implementation, the help files can  only
2140 ' be read sequentially and must all be printed before a return
2150 ' to the Notebook menu takes place.  Relatively simply changes
2160 ' could   be   made  to  provide  access  to  each  help  file
2170 ' inidividually.
2180 '
2190 CLS
2200 PRINT"      NOTEBOOK/BAS is a simple file system designed to  main-"
2210 PRINT"tain  data  on disk.  It is patterned after the PERCOM NOTE-"
2220 PRINT"BOOK running under OS-80.  A 'page' of  data  is  simply  15"
2230 PRINT"lines  on  the  screen.  It may contain anything that you can"
2240 PRINT"type in.  Simple commands allow  the  data  to  be  entered,"
2250 PRINT"retrieved, and deleted.  "
2260 AE$=CHR$(13)
2270 PM$="<ENTER>"
2280 GOSUB 7050
2290 PRINT"      The 'READ' command causes pages of data to be read from"
2300 PRINT"the disk and displayed on the screen.  As each page is  read"
2310 PRINT"the  system  will  flash '<<--, -->, X>'.  Entry of the left"
2320 PRINT"arrow will cause the previous page to  be  displayed,  while"
2330 PRINT"the right arrow will display the next page.  An entry of 'X'"
```

```
2340 PRINT"will  terminate the display and return to the menu.  If Page"
2350 PRINT"0 is requested, the Table of Contents will be displayed.  "
2360 GOSUB 7050
2370 PRINT"      The 'WRITE' function allows data to be entered into the"
2380 PRINT"system.  Data is entered a line at a time, up to  15  lines."
2390 PRINT"If  no  data  is  entered for a line, the page is considered"
2400 PRINT"finished and is written to disk.  Thus, to put blank  lines"
2410 PRINT"in  a  page,  at least one space must be entered.  An entire"
2420 PRINT"page may be deleted by hitting <ENTER>  at  the  prompt  for"
2430 PRINT"Line  1.   By specifying Page 0 the Table of Contents may be"
2440 PRINT"updated.  "
2450 GOSUB 7050
2460 PRINT"      GETFILE allows the user to enter a prepared  text  file"
2470 PRINT"from  disk  into  the  current NOTEBOOK.  The GETFILE option"
```

```
2480 PRINT"will first ask for FILESPECS for  the  disk  file  following"
2490 PRINT"standard  TRSDOS conventions.  The user must insure that the"
2500 PRINT"disk file contains no more than fifteen lines and that  each"
2510 PRINT"line  is  no longer that 63 characters.  The GETFILE routine"
2520 PRINT"will truncate longer lines to 63 characters  and  will  read"
2530 PRINT"only the first 15 lines.  This option allows the preparation"
2540 PRINT"of a file with a text editor and/or text formatter.  "
2550 GOSUB 7050
2560 PRINT"     The 'NEW' function will cause the entire NOTEBOOK to be"
2570 PRINT"initialized to a blank state.  This function should  not  be"
2580 PRINT"invoked  before making a copy of the NOTEBOOK file if one by"
2590 PRINT"the same name already exists.  "
2600 PRINT" "
2610 PRINT"     'HELP' prints out this text.  'EXIT' takes you back  to"
2620 PRINT"the system level (DOS or BASIC).  "
2630 GOSUB 7050
2640 RETURN
2650 '
3000 '                   Subroutine - READ Function
3010 '
3020 ' Purpose - To  read  and  display  pages  of  the  NOTEBOOK.
3030 '     Although  <PAGE> is optional, the function READ requested
3040 '     without a page number will print the Table of Contents as
3050 '     will the command, READ 0.
3060 '
3070 ' Subroutines Used -
3080 '
3090 '     Bottom of Page Routine
3100 '     Load Table of Contents
3110 '
3120 ' Notes -
3130 '
3140 '     READ <PAGE> allows the user to read the page specified.
3150 ' If one note requires more than one page, only the first page
3160 ' of the note should be entered in the Table of  Contents  and
3170 ' the  user  should use the right arrow key (-->) and the left
3180 ' arrow key (<--) to move to the previous or the next page.
3190 '
3200 GOSUB 8070 ' GET PAGE NUMBER
3210 IF PG=0 THEN 3420  ' READ TABLE OF CONTENTS
3220 '
```

==

```
3230 ' Read the designated page of the notebook (PG).
3240 '
3250 CLS
3260 PRINT @ 0,"";
3270 FOR I=0 TO 3
3280 II=I+1
3290 GET 1, FN SC(PG)+II
3300 B$(I)=BF$
3310 IF I<>3 THEN 3330
3320 B$(I)=LEFT$(B$(I), LEN(B$(I))-64)
3330 PRINT B$(I);
3340 NEXT I
```

```
3350 PRINT @ 960,"PAGE";PG;
3360 GOSUB 6050
3370 IF FN UL$(CE$)="X" THEN RETURN
3380 GOTO 3210
3390 '
3400 ' Get and print the Table of Contents page.
3410 '
3420 CLS
3430 PRINT FN CE$("NOTEBOOK - TABLE OF CONTENTS",64);
3440 PRINT
3450 GOSUB 9040 ' Load the Table of Contents
3460 FOR I=0 TO 3
3470 PRINT @ 128+I*16,"ITEM        PAGE";
3480 FOR J=0 TO 11
3490 IF TC(I*12+J)<=0 THEN 3350
3500 PRINT @ 192+I*16+J*64, TC$(I*12+J);
3510 PRINT USING " ####";TC(I*12+J);
3520 NEXT J
3530 NEXT I
3540 GOTO 3350
3550 '
4000 '                  Subroutine - WRITE Function
4010 '
4020 ' Purpose - To write  a  new  page  to  the  notebook.   This
4030 '     function  is  used to write a page of notes as well as to
4040 '     write entries to the Table of Contents.   The   syntax   is
4050 '     WRITE <PAGE> where <PAGE> is an optional page number.   If
4060 '     no  page number is specified, the default is to the Table
4070 '     of Contents.
4080 '
4090 ' Subroutines Used -
4100 '
4110 '     Get Page Number (to be written)
4120 '     Get a Disk File (GETFILE)
4130 '     Bottom of Page Routine
4140 '
4150 ' Notes -
4160 '
4170 '       The WRITE function is called regardless of  the  source
4180 ' of  the notes (the keyboard or a disk file).  If the note is
4190 ' to come from a text file, the disk file routine  is  called,
4200 ' otherwise  the  keyboard  entry routine is used.  If the page
4210 ' number to be written is zero, a branch is made to the  Table
```

A NOTEBOOK PROGRAM   DATE- TIME-
==

```
4220 ' of  Contents   routine   which   is   part of the write function
4230 ' subroutine.
4240 '
4250 IF GT THEN 4290
4260 GOSUB 8070    ' GET THE PAGE NUMBER
4270 IF MP=0 THEN RETURN
4280 IF PG=0 THEN 4580
4290 FOR I=0 TO 15
   : LN$(I)="": NEXT I
4300 IF GT THEN GOSUB 11070
```

```
           : GOTO 4440   ' GET A DISK FILE
4310 CLS
4320 PRINT @ 960,"ENTER PAGE";PG; CHR$(30);
4330 FOR I=0 TO 14
4340 PRINT @ I*64, USING "##";I+1;
4350 PRINT CHR$(30);
4360 LINE INPUT LN$(I)
4370 IF LEN(LN$(I))<64 THEN 4410
4380 PRINT @ 960,"LAST LINE WAS TOO LONG!  RE-ENTER";CHR$(30);
4390 LN$(I)=""
4400 GOTO 4340
4410 IF LEN(LN$(I))=0 THEN 4440
4420 LN$(I)=LN$(I)+CHR$(13)
4430 NEXT I
4440 FOR I=0 TO 3
4450 BX$=""
4460 FOR J=0 TO 3
4470 BX$=BX$+LN$(I*4+J)
4480 NEXT J
4490 BX$=BX$+STRING$(255-LEN(BX$), 0)
4500 II=I+1
4510 LSET BF$=BX$
4520 PUT 1, FN SC(PG)+II
4530 NEXT I
4540 GOSUB 6050
4550 IF FN UL$(CE$)="X" THEN RETURN
4560 GOTO 4280
4570 '
4580 ' MAKE ENTRY IN TABLE OF CONTENTS
4590 '
4600 CLS
4610 PRINT "TABLE OF CONTENTS UPDATE"
4620 PRINT
4630 GOSUB 9040 ' Load Table of Contents
4640 PRINT "ENTER KEYWORD (8 CHARACTERS OR LESS) OR 'ENTER' TO EXIT"
4650 KY$=""
4660 INPUT KY$
4670 IF KY$="" THEN GOSUB 10040
     : RETURN
4680 IF LEN(KY$)>8 THEN 4640
4690 KW$=LEFT$(KY$+"        ",8)
4700 FOR I=0 TO 47
4710 IF TC(I)=0 THEN 4750
4720 IF TC$(I)=KW$ THEN 4830
4730 IF TC$(I)>KW$ THEN 4750
```

===

```
4740 NEXT I
4750 PRINT KY$;" NOT IN TABLE OF CONTENTS."
4760 QA$=""
4770 INPUT "WANT TO ADD IT";QA$
4780 IF FN UL$(QA$)<>"Y" THEN 4640
4790 IF TC(47)>0 THEN PRINT "TABLE FULL!  CANNOT ADD!"
     : GOTO 4640
```

```
4800 FOR J=47 TO I+1 STEP-1
     : TC$(J)=TC$(J-1)
     : TC(J)=TC(J-1)
     : NEXT J
4810 TC$(I)=KW$
4820 GOTO 4880
4830 PRINT KY$;" REFERS TO PAGE";TC(I);"."
4840 QA$=""
4850 INPUT "WANT TO CHANGE OR DELETE IT";QA$
4860 IF FN UL$(QA$)="Y" THEN 4880
4870 GOTO 4580
4880 INPUT "ENTER PAGE NUMBER (0 TO DELETE)";PG
4890 IF PG=0 THEN 4940
4900 IF PG<0 OR PG>MP THEN 4880
4910 TC(I)=PG
4920 GOTO 4640
4930 IF I=47 THEN 4950
4940 FOR J=I TO 46: TC$(J)=TC$(J+1): TC(J)=TC(J+1)
     : NEXT J
4950 TC$(J)=""
4960 TC(J)=0
4970 GOTO 4640
4980 '
5000 '                    Subroutine - NEW Function
5010 '
5020 ' Purpose - To initialize a  NEW  notebook  by  writing  ascii
5030 '     zeros to all pages and disk locations of the notebook.
5040 '
5050 ' Subroutines Used -
5060 '
5070 '     None.
5080 '
5090 ' Notes -
5100 '
5110 '       The purpose of initializing an entire notebook  at  its
5120 ' inception  is  twofold.  First, all appropriate segments of
5130 ' the disk will be zeroed out.  This will mean  that  for  any
5140 ' READ of  a  page, that page will contain only what the user
5150 ' has placed on that page.  Second, by  prior  initialization,
5160 ' the disk access time will be a little faster.
5170 '
5180 CLS
5190 INPUT "NUMBER OF PAGES";LS
5200 LS=LS*4+4
5210 PRINT "FOR";((LS-FS+1)-4)/4;" PAGES."
5220 PRINT
5230 BX$=STRING$(255, CHR$(0))
5240 FOR I=1 TO 4
```

```
5250 LSET BF$=BX$
5260 PUT 1, I
5270 NEXT I
5280 BX$=""
```

```
5290 FOR I=5 TO LS
5300 LSET BF$=BX$
5310 PUT 1, I
5320 NEXT I
5330 CLOSE 1
     : OPEN "R",1,FI$
5340 RETURN
5350 '
6000 '              Subroutine - Bottom of Page for Notebook
6010 '
6020 ' Purpose - To provide an appropriate bottom of page  (screen)
6030 '     routine for the Notebook page display.
6040 '
6050 PM$="<" +LA$+", " +RA$+", X>"
6060 AE$=CHR$(8)+CHR$(9)+"X"
6070 GOSUB 7050
6080 IF FN UL$(CE$)="X" THEN RETURN
6090 IF CE$=CHR$(8) AND PG>0 THEN PG=PG-1
     : RETURN
6100 IF CE$=CHR$(9) AND PG+1<MP THEN PG=PG+1
     : RETURN
6110 RETURN
6120 '
7000 '              Subroutine - Flash Prompt, Get Character
7010 '
7020 ' Purpose - To flash a prompt at  the  user,  then  capture  a
7030 '     character from the keyboard when the user responds.
7040 '
7050 LP=INT((64-LEN(PM$))/2)
7060 PRINT @ 960+LP, PM$;
7070 FOR XX=1 TO 100
7080 NEXT XX
7090 PRINT @ 960+LP, STRING$(LEN(PM$)," ");
7100 FOR XX=1 TO 100
7110 NEXT XX
7120 CE$=INKEY$
7130 IF CE$="" THEN 7060
7140 CLS
7150 RETURN
7160 '
8000 '              Subroutine - Get Page Number from Function Line
8010 '
8020 ' Purpose - To  get  an  appropriate  page  number  from  the
8030 '     function  line  in  the  event that a page number has not
8040 '     been specified when a read  or  write  command  has  been
8050 '     given.
8060 '
8070 PG=VAL(MID$(FC$, LEN(PR$(J))))
8080 IF PG>=0 AND PG<MP THEN RETURN
8090 IF PG>MP THEN 8100 ELSE 8130
8100 PRINT FNCE$("*** YOU MUST USE THE 'NEW' COMMAND ***",64)
```

```
8110 FOR I=1 TO 500: NEXT I
8120 RETURN
8130 INPUT "PAGE NUMBER";PG
```

```
8140 GOTO 8080
8150 '
9000 '                    Subroutine - Load Table of Contents
9010 '
9020 ' Purpose - To load the current Table of Contents from Disk.
9030 '
9040 IF TC(0)>0 THEN RETURN
9050 FOR I=0 TO 1
9060 GET 1, FS+I
9070 FOR J=0 TO 23
9080 FIELD #1,(10*J) AS XX$, 8 AS WD$, 2 AS PL$
9090 TC$(I*24+J)=WD$
9100 TC(I*24+J)=CVI(PL$)
9110 NEXT J
9120 NEXT I
9130 RETURN
9140 '
10000 '               Subroutine - Write the Table of Contents
10010 '
10020 ' Purpose - To write the updated Table of Contents to Disk.
10030 '
10040 LSET BF$=STRING$(250, CHR$(0))
10050 FOR I=1 TO 4
10060 PUT 1, I
10070 NEXT I
10080 FOR I=0 TO 1
10090 FOR J=0 TO 23
10100 FIELD #1,(10*J) AS XX$, 8 AS WD$, 2 AS PL$
10110 LSET WD$=TC$(I*24+J)
10120 LSET PL$=MKI$(TC(I*24+J))
10130 NEXT J
10140 PUT 1, FS+I
10150 NEXT I
10160 RETURN
10170 '
11000 '                    Subroutine - Get a Disk File
11010 '
11020 ' Purpose - To get a notebook page from  an  already  prepared
11030 '    disk   file.    This   routine,   called   from   the   Write
11040 '    subroutine, implements the GETFILE command  which  is  an
11050 '    extension of the original version of NOTEBOOK.
11060 '
11070 CLS
11080 FOR I=0 TO 15
11090 LN$(I)=""
11100 NEXT I
11110 LINE INPUT "ENTER FILESPECS <FILENM/EXT:D#>: ";FI$
11120 INPUT "PAGE NUMBER";PG
11130 CLS
11140 OPEN "I",2, FI$
11150 J=0
11160 IF EOF(2) THEN 11240
```

```
11170 LINE INPUT #2, LN$(J)
11180 IF LEN(LN$(J))>63 THEN LN$(J)=LEFT$(LN$(J), 63)
```

```
11190 PRINT LN$(J)
11200 LN$(J)=LN$(J)+CHR$(13)
11210 J=J+1
11220 IF J=16 THEN 11240
11230 GOTO 11160
11240 CLOSE 2
11250 RETURN
```

==

Listing 4
A Disk Management Program

```
100 '                    A Disk Management Program
110 '                         by Thomas Wm. Madron
120 '
130 '  The idea for this program originated in Bud Baker,
140 '    "Dirpick," TRS-80 MICROCOMPUTER NEWS, July 1981, p. 8.
150 '    Those portions of the original program still retained are
160 '    used by permission of Bud Baker.
170 '
180 '       Whenever a computer system with any external storage
190 '  device is used it will be necessary, sooner or later, to
200 '  exert some effort managing the way in which storage space is
210 '  used.  The intent of this program, called by the main MENU
220 '  program, is to make the management of diskette space as
230 '  simple and easy as possible.  When called, the user is asked
240 '  to enter a drive number (on the TRS-80 from 0-3).   The
250 '  program then lists the names of the files on the specified
260 '  drive, sorting them in alphabetical order, and appending a
270 '  number to each one, thus resulting in a comprehensive menu
280 '  addressing all the files on the diskette.
290 '
300 '       When the menu of disk files has been printed on the
310 '  screen, the program then prints an action menu which allows
320 '  the user to do several things with any or all files.  If a
330 '  file is another program, in machine language (/CMD), BASIC
340 '  (/BAS), or structured as a DO file, it can be executed
350 '  directly.  Files can also be killed (erased) or copied.  It
360 '  is also possible to select another disk for review, return
370 '  to BASIC, or go to the disk operating system.  When the
380 '  program is complete (except, of course, if another program
390 '  was executed), control returns to the main MENU program.
100 '  Thus, for many disk management problems, it is never
410 '  necessary to leave the system of programs.
420 '
430 '       Baker's original program implemented, in a fashion
440 '  quite different from the current program, a disk directory
450 '  menu which allowed the execution of any program files.   It
460 '  was not a general purpose disk management program.
470 '  Especially in the way in which the disk directory is
480 '  accessed this program differs markedly from Baker's.  Baker
490 '  used the built-in function CMD"D:n" (built into the TRS-80
500 '  Model III), where "n" is the drive number.  While Baker's
510 '  technique will work most of the time, there are instances
520 '  when it will not.  A more stable and faster approach is to
```

```
530 ' directly read the disk directory and print it.  The  methods
540 ' for  using  the TRS-80 disk handling routines, as documented
550 ' in the Model III OWNER'S MANUAL, can be found in  Harold  B.
560 ' Fink,  "Direct  Access,"  80-MICROCOMPUTING, April 1982, pp.
570 ' 214-219.
580 '
590 ' Subroutines Used -
600 '
```

A DISK MANAGEMENT PROGRAM   DATE- TIME-
===

```
610 '     Execute a Designated Program (Line 2000)
620 '     Kill Files (Line 3000)
630 '     Variable List Decoder (Line 4000)
640 '     Copy Files (Line 5000)
650 '     Print Header (Line 6000)
660 '     Read and Print a Disk Directory (Line 7000)
670 '
680 '         Load Register Information (Line 8000)
690 '         Execute Call to $RAMDIR (Line 9000)
700 '
710 '     Set Memory Protection for Directory Buffer (Line 10000)
720 '     Restore Memory Protection (Line 11000)
730 '     Initialize Directory Buffer (Line 12000)
740 '     Load Directory Calling Machine Language Routine
750 '         (Line 13000)
760 '     Load Buffer Initialization Machine Language Routine
770 '         (Line 14000)
780 '
790 ' Notes -
800 '
810 '     During its operation DSKMGT/BAS resets  BASIC's  memory
820 ' size  in  order  to  protect a buffer which will contain the
830 ' disk directory.  When the program is  exited,  the  original
840 ' memory size is restored.
850 '
860 ' INITIALIZE DSKMGT RUN
870 '
880 CLEAR 5000: DEFINT A-L,N-W: IX=0
890 DIM RT(16),PR$(96),LV(96),V(16)
900 ND=96: ' MAX NUMBER OF DIRECTORY ENTRIES
910 DEFFNCE$(A$,N)=STRING$(FIX((N-LEN(A$))/2)," ")+A$
920 DEF FNMOD(X,Y)=INT(Y*(X/Y-INT(X/Y))+.001)
930 DEF FNXU(X)=X+65536!*(X>32767)
940 POKE 16419,32 ' Set Cursor Character to Blank
950 GOSUB 13170: ' LOAD DIRECTORY CALLING ROUTINE
960 GOSUB 14140: ' LOAD BUFFER INITIALIZATION ROUTINE
970 '
980 ' Protect 2561 bytes of memory for Directory Buffer
990 '
1000 GOSUB 10170 ' SET MEMORY SIZE
1010 GOSUB 6050 ' PRINT HEADER
1020 PRINT "ENTER DRIVE NUMBER (0-3) OR <ENTER> TO EXIT: ";
1030 DR$=INKEY$
    : IF DR$="" THEN 1030  ELSE PRINT DR$
1040 IF DR$=CHR$(13) THEN CLS
```

```
      : GOSUB 11050
      : RUN "MENU/BAS"
1050 IF DR$<"0" OR DR$>"3" THEN 1020  ELSE DR=VAL(DR$)
1060 '
1070 ' Get and Print Disk Directory, then Print Action Menu
1080 '
1090 GOSUB 7250 ' GET AND PRINT DISK DIRECTORY
1100 PRINT @ 704,FNCE$("SELECT FUNCTION BY NUMBER:",64)
1110 PRINT "(1) EXECUTE A PROGRAM";TAB(32);"(2) KILL ONE OR MORE FILES"
1120 PRINT "(3) COPY ONE OR MORE FILES";TAB(32);"(4) RETURN TO DOS"
```

A DISK MANAGEMENT PROGRAM   DATE- TIME-
==

```
1130 PRINT "(5) SELECT ANOTHER DISK";TAB(32);"(6) RETURN TO BASIC"
1140 PRINT FNCE$("WHICH FUNCTION? ",64);CHR$(14);
1150 POKE 16419,176 ' RESTORE CURSOR CHARACTER
1160 Y$=INKEY$
      : IF Y$="" THEN 1160
1170 IF VAL(Y$)<1 OR VAL(Y$)>6 THEN 1160
1180 POKE 16419,32 ' SET CURSOR TO BLANK
1190 PRINT Y$;CHR$(15);
      : PRINT @ 704,CHR$(31);
1200 ON VAL(Y$) GOTO 1210 ,1220 ,1230 ,1240 ,1260 ,1250
1210 GOSUB 2240
      : GOTO 1260 ' EXECUTE DESIGNATED PROGRAM
1220 GOSUB 3200
      : GOTO 1260 ' KILL FILES
1230 GOSUB 5260
      : GOTO 1260 ' COPY FILES
1240 GOSUB 11050
      : CMD "S"
1250 CLS: GOSUB 11050
      : END
1260 GOSUB 11050
      : RUN
1270 '
2000 '              Subroutine - Execute Designated Program
2010 '
2020 ' Purpose - To take a program (file)  name  contained  in  the
2030 '     array  PR$(i) and execute it, depending on its particular
2040 '     type.
2050 '
2060 ' Notes -
2070 '
2080 '       There  are  several  types  of  files  which  might  be
2090 ' executed  on  a TRS-80 including those ending in /CMD, /BAS,
2100 ' and /BLD.  /CMD files are machine language programs and  are
2110 ' executed  directly  under TRSDOS by simply typing the name of
2120 ' the program.  Such programs can also be executed from  BASIC
2130 ' with  the  TRS-80 built-in function, CMD"I","filename".  /BAS
2140 ' files  are  BASIC  programs  and  are  executed  from BASIC by
2150 ' simply  issuing  the command RUN "filename".  /BLD files are
2160 ' executed from TRSDOS by the DO  command.    /BLD  files  are
2170 ' usually  composed  of a "job stream"--that is, several TRSDOS
2180 ' and/or other programs and files.  The DO program is called a
2190 ' command  processor  and  is  similar to the  SUBMIT  command  in
```

102

```
2200 ' CP/M.  If this program was being converted to run under CP/M
2210 ' it  would  be  necessary  to  also  change  the way in which
2220 ' machine language programs were executed from BASIC.
2230 '
2240 INPUT "ENTER PROGRAM NUMBER (0 TO RESTART)";X
2250 IF X=0 THEN GOSUB 11050: RUN
2260 IF INSTR(PR$(X),"/BLD") THEN IX=1
     : GOSUB 11050
     : CMD "I","DO "+PR$(X)
2270 IF INSTR(PR$(X),"/CMD") THEN IX=1
     : GOSUB 11050
     : CMD "I",PR$(X)
```

```
2280 IF INSTR(PR$(X),"/BAS") THEN IX=1
     : GOSUB 11050
     : RUN PR$(X)
2290 CLS
     : PRINT PR$(X);" is not an executable file"
2300 PRINT @ 960,FNCE$("Press ANY key to continue",64);
2310 IF INKEY$="" THEN 2310 ELSE RETURN
2320 '
3000 '                    Subroutine - Kill Files
3010 '
3020 ' Purpose - To allow one or more files to be killed or erased.
3030 '
3040 ' Subroutines Used -
3050 '
3060 '       Variable List Decoder
3070 '
3080 ' Notes -
3090 '
3100 '        The convenience of this command lies in the fact that a
3110 ' list of file numbers, listed either as  a  range  (1-5,  for
3120 ' example),  or  as  a  string  of numbers separated by commas
3130 ' (1,2,3,4,5 for example), or  some  combination  of  the  two
3140 ' styles,  can be used for designating files to be killed.  It
3150 ' is sometimes necessary to clean large numbers of files off a
3160 ' disk and this provides a method easier to use than even  the
3170 ' PURGE  command  in TRSDOS.  It can be a dangerous command to
3180 ' use, however, so be careful!
3190 '
3200 PRINT "LIST FILE NUMBERS TO BE KILLED (0 TO RESTART): "
3210 GOSUB 4350 : ' GET NUMBER LIST
3220 IF LV(0)=0 THEN RETURN
3230 FOR I=0 TO NV-1
3240 PRINT @ 960,FNCE$("*** Killing "+PR$(LV(I))+" ***",64);
3250 KILL PR$(LV(I))
3260 PRINT @ 960,CHR$(30);
3270 NEXT I
3280 RETURN
3290 '
4000 '            Subroutine - Variable List Decoder (2)
4010 '
4020 ' PURPOSE - To read a string from the keyboard composed of
```

```
4030 '    numbers, commas, and/or hyphens and to return a
4040 '    vector containing the numbers stated or implied.
4050 '
4060 ' Important Variables:
4070 '
4080 '    NV:      Total number of values returned.
4090 '
4100 '    LV(I):   Array containing the vector of values read.
4110 '
4120 ' Notes:
4130 '
4140 '    This routine allows for the input of a string of
4150 ' numbers on a single line without the need for specifying
4160 ' an explicit number of variables (as with the INPUT
```

```
4170 ' statement in BASIC).    When using the subroutine to
4180 ' process a string of integers (returned in LV(I)), each
4190 ' of the following is acceptable:
4200 '
4210 '    1,2,3,4,5
4220 '
4230 '    1-5
4240 '
4250 '    1-3,4,5
4260 '
4270 '    In each of the illustrations LV(I) (locations 0-4)
4280 ' would return with the number 1 to 5 and NV would = 5.  A
4290 ' string of continuous and contiguous number can be
4300 ' entered using the beginning and ending number separated
4310 ' by a hyphen.   Thus, 1-5 means a string of numbers
4320 ' consisting of the integers 1 to 5 inclusive of both 1
4330 ' and 5.  A carriage return <ENTER> terminates the string.
4340 '
4350 V$="":V1$="":K=0
     :L1=0
     :L2=0
     :NV=0
4360 POKE 16419,176
     : PRINT "ENTER NUMBER LIST: ":LINEINPUT V$
4370 IF LEN(V$)=0 THEN RETURN
4380 ' SEARCH FOR INDIVIDUAL VARIABLES
4390 L1=INSTR(V$,",")
4400 IF L1>0 THEN V1$=LEFT$(V$,L1-1)
     : V$=MID$(V$,L1+1)
4410 IF L1=0 THEN V1$=V$
     : V$=""
4420 L2=INSTR(V1$,"-")
4430 IF L2 THEN 4460
4440 LV(K)=VAL(V1$): K=K+1
     : NV=K
     : GOTO 4370
4450 ' BEGIN LOOP FOR CONTIGUOUS VARS
4460 V2=VAL(MID$(V1$,1,3))
     : V3=VAL(MID$(V1$,L2+1,3))
```

104

```
4470 FOR I=V2 TO V3
    :LV(K)=I
    :K=K+1
    :NEXT I
4480 NV=K
    :GOTO 4370
4490 '
5000 '                    Subroutine - Copy Files
5010 '
5020 ' Purpose - To provide a generalized method for copying  files
5030 '     from one disk to another or from one disk file to another
5040 '     on the same disk.
5050 '
5060 ' Notes -
5070 '
5080 '        This subroutine uses a  somewhat  inelegant  method  of
```

===

```
5090 ' copying  files.   There are problems with copying some types
5100 ' of files with BASIC input and output statements,  especially
5110 ' machine  language  files.    Consequently,   the  TRSDOS copy
5120 ' command  is  used  to  do  the  copying.   In   order   to
5130 ' accomplish  this,  a  DO  file  is built as a temporary disk
5140 ' file, TMP/BLD.  The next to the last line of the DO file  is
5150 ' one  which kills the temporary file itself.  By the time the
5160 ' DO file has executed  the  kill  command,  however,  it  has
5170 ' already  placed  the final line of the DO file in the buffer
5180 ' to be executed, and that is a command to RUN the  DSKMGT/BAS
5190 ' program  again.   Thus,  the  logic of this subroutine is to
5200 ' build a DO file, exit to TRSDOS to execute the DO file,  and
5210 ' as  a  last command of the DO file, rerun the disk management
5220 ' program.  The consequence of this  approach  is  that  there
5230 ' must  be  some  small  amount  of disk space available, on a
5240 ' temporary basis, for the DO file named TMP/BLD.
5250 '
5260 PRINT "COPY FILE FROM DRIVE";DR;" TO DRIVE";
    :INPUT D2
5270 IF D2<0 OR D2>3 THEN 5260
5280 PRINT "ENTER FILES TO BE COPIED BY NUMBER (0 TO RESTART):"
5290 GOSUB 4350 : ' GET VARIABLE LIST
5300 IF LV(0)=0 THEN RETURN
5310 OPEN "O",1,"TMP/BLD:0"
5320 FOR I=0 TO NV-1
5330 PRINT #1,"COPY ";PR$(LV(I));" :";MID$(STR$(D2),2)
5340 NEXT I
5350 PRINT #1,"BASIC"
5360 PRINT #1," "
5370 PRINT #1," "
5380 PRINT #1,"KILL "+CHR$(34)+"TMP/BLD"+CHR$(34)
5390 PRINT #1," RUN "+CHR$(34)+"DSKMGT/BAS"+CHR$(34)
5400 CLOSE 1
5410 CMD"I","DO TMP"
5420 RETURN
5430 '
6000 '                    Subroutine - Print Header
```

```
6010 '
6020 ' Purpose - To print a standardized header for the Disk
6030 '     Management Program.
6040 '
6050 CLS ' CLEAR THE SCREEN
6060 PRINT FNCE$("DISK MANAGEMENT",64)
6070 PRINT STRING$(64,131);
6080 RETURN
6090 '
7000 '          Subroutine - Read and Print a Disk Directory
7010 '
7020 ' Purpose - To read the disk directory sector, format it
7030 '     appropriately, and print the directory on the Screen.
7040 '
7050 ' Subroutines Used -
7060 '
7070 '     Protect Upper Memory
7080 '     Set Parameters for Call to RAMDIR$
```

===

```
7090 '     Execute Machine Language Routine
7100 '
7110 ' Notes -
7120 '
7130 '     This subroutine establishes a call to $RAMDIR, the
7140 ' TRSDOS subroutine which accesses a disk directory. The
7150 ' technique for initializing $RAMDIR and doing the call is
7160 ' described in Harold B. Fink, "Direct Access," 80-
7170 ' MICROCOMPUTING, April 1982, p. 214. Directory records are
7180 ' loaded into a string array, PR$(i), which is then sorted in
7190 ' alphabetical order using the built-in command, CMD
7200 ' "O",n,stringarray. Similar techniques can probably be used
7210 ' to access appropriate routines in CP/M, although a sort
7220 ' subroutine would have to be included in the program for
7230 ' other operating systems. The directory is then printed.
7240 '
7250 CLS: RM=22
   : 'RAM DIRECTORY RECORD LENGTH
7260 BF$=STRING$(RM,32) 'SET UP BUFFER & LOAD WITH BLANKS
7270 '
7280 GOSUB 11050
   : ' RESTORE MEMORY PROTECTION
7290 GOSUB 10170
   : ' PROTECT UPPER MEMORY
7300 GOSUB 8080
   : ' SET PARAMETERS FOR CALL TO $RAMDIR
7310 GOSUB 9060
   : ' EXECUTE M/L ROUTINE
7320 '
7330 ' PUT DIRECTORY INFO IN PR$()
7340 '
7350 ZX=Z3
   : TS=1
7360 FOR I=1 TO ND
   : BF$=STRING$(RM-TS,32)
   : M2=VARPTR(BF$)
```

```
7370 POKE M2+1,FNMOD(ZX,256)
   : POKE M2+2,INT(ZX/256)
7380 IF INSTR(BF$,"/")=0 THEN TS=1 ELSE TS=0
7390 ZX=ZX+(RM-TS)
7400 II=INSTR(BF$,":")
   : IF II=0 THEN JJ=I
   : I=0
   : GOTO 7460
7410 IF LEFT$(BF$,1)=" " GOSUB 7630
7420 PR$(I)=BF$: NEXT I
7430 '
7440 ' SORT PR$()
7450 '
7460 IF JJ=1 THEN 7470 ELSE 7490
7470 PRINT FNCE$("*** NO FILES ON DRIVE"+STR$(DR)+" ***",64)
7480 RETURN
7490 JJ=JJ-1
   : CMD"O",JJ,PR$(1)
7500 '
```

A DISK MANAGEMENT PROGRAM   DATE- TIME-
===

```
7510 ' PRINT DIRECTORY
7520 '
7530 PRINT "DRIVE NUMBER: ";DR
7540 FOR J=1 TO JJ STEP 4: K=J+3
   : IF K>JJ THEN K=JJ
7550 FOR L=J TO K
7560 AA$=LEFT$(PR$(L),INSTR(PR$(L),":")-1)
   : PR$(L)=AA$+":"+MID$(STR$(DR),2)
7570 AA$=LEFT$(AA$,11)
7580 PRINT USING "## %            % ";L;AA$;
7590 NEXT L
7600 PRINT
7610 NEXT J
7620 RETURN
7630 IF LEFT$(BF$,1)=" " THEN BF$=MID$(BF$,2)
   : GOTO 7630
7640 RETURN
7650 '
8000 '          Subroutine - Load Registers with Parameters
8010 '
8020 ' Purpose - To  load  specified  registers  with  informations
8030 '    necessary  for  the execution of $RAMDIR.  HL=Ram Buffer;
8040 '    C=option switch; B=specified drive number.
8050 '
8060 ' LOAD BUFFER ADDRESS INTO HL REGISTERS
8070 '
8080 RT(3)=FNMOD(Z1,256)
   : RT(4)=INT(Z1/256)
8090 '
8100 RT(6)=DR
   : 'LOAD DRIVE NUMBER INTO B
8110 RT(8)=0
   : 'FUNCTION SWITCH IN C, 0=ENTIRE DIRECTORY
8120 RT(10)=FNMOD(17040,256)
```

```
     : RT(11)=INT(17040/256)
     : '$RAMDIR
8130 ' GET EXIT ADDRESS OF DIRECTORY
8140 RT(13)=FNMOD(Z1-2,256)
     : RT(14)=INT((Z1-2)/256)
8150 '
8160 ' SET UP ROUTINE IN STRING RT$
8170 '
8180 RT$="": FOR I=1 TO 16
     : RT$=RT$+CHR$(RT(I))
     : NEXT I
8190 RETURN
8200 '
9000 '                    Subroutine - Execute $RAMDIR
9010 '
9020 ' Purpose - To find the address of string RT$  containing  the
9030 '    machine  language  calling  program of $RAMDIR, which, in
9040 '    turn, executes $RAMDIR.
9050 '
9060 M1=PEEK(VARPTR(RT$)+2)*256+PEEK(VARPTR(RT$)+1)
9070 M1=FNXU(M1)
```

==

```
9080 DEFUSR1=M1
     : X=USR1(0)
9090 Z3=PEEK(FNXU(Z1-1))*256+PEEK(FNXU(Z1-2))
9100 RETURN
9110 '
10000 '             Subroutine - Protect Upper Memory
10010 '
10020 ' Purpose - To provide a means for respecifying 'memory  size'
10030 '    from BASIC.
10040 '
10050 ' Notes -
10060 '
10070 '      Memory  size,  as  set  by  the  user  when  BASIC  is
10080 ' initialized,  is  kept,  on  the TRS-80 Model III, in memory
10090 ' locations &H40B1 and &H40B2.  This can be changed from BASIC
10100 ' by poking other values.  40B1 contains the LSB of  the  top
10110 ' address  space, and 40B2 contains the MSB of the top address
10120 ' space.  Z2 retains the old upper limit, Z1  the  new.   The
10130 ' amount required by $RAMDIR is 2561+64 bytes.
10140 '
10150 ' PROTECT UPPER 2561 + 64 BYTES OF MEMORY
10160 '
10170 Z2=(PEEK(&H40B2)*256+PEEK(&H40B1))
10180 Z1=Z2-(2561+64)
10190 POKE &H40B1,FNMOD(Z1-4,256)
     : POKE &H40B2,INT((Z1-4)/256)
10200 RETURN
10210 '
11000 '             Subroutine - Restore Memory Protection
11010 '
11020 ' Purpose - To  restore  original  memory  protections  before
11030 '    exiting DSKMGT/BAS.
11040 '
```

```
11050 POKE &H40B1,FNMOD(Z2,256)
   : POKE &H40B2,INT(Z2/256)
11060 POKE 16419,176
   : 'RESTORE CURSOR
11070 IF IX=1 THEN IX=0
   : RETURN
11080 GOSUB 12160
   : ' INITIALIZE BUFFER AREA TO ZEROS
11090 RETURN
11100 '
12000 '          Subroutine - Initialize Directory Buffer Area
12010 '
12020 ' Purpose - To initialize the buffer area required by  $RAMDIR
12030 '     for storing a disk directory file.
12040 '
12050 ' Notes -
12060 '
12070 '     A buffer of 2560+1 bytes of memory is required to  hold
12080 ' the directory records for later use by the program.  Between
12090 ' directory  reads  the  buffer  must  be  initialized (set to
12100 ' zero).  Although  the  initialization  can  be  accomplished
12110 ' directly in BASIC, such initialization tends to be slow.  As
```

```
12120 ' a  consequence,  a  short  machine language program is used.
12130 ' This subroutine sets parameter values for the routine,  then
12140 ' executes the program.
12150 '
12160 ZE$="": V(3)=FNMOD(Z1,256)
   : V(4)=INT(Z1/256)
   : 'BUFFER ADDRESS
12170 V(6)=V(3)+1
   : V(7)=V(4)
   : 'NEXT ADDRESS
12180 FOR I=1 TO 16
   : ZE$=ZE$+CHR$(V(I))
   : NEXT I
12190 MZ=PEEK(VARPTR(ZE$)+2)*256+PEEK(VARPTR(ZE$)+1)
12200 MZ=FNXU(MZ)
   : DEFUSR2=MZ
   : A=USR2(0)
   : RETURN
12210 '
13000 '          Subroutine - Load $RAMDIR M/L Calling Routine
13010 '
13020 ' Purpose - To load the machine language  program  which  does
13030 '     the actual call to $RAMDIR into array RT(i).
13040 '
13050 ' Notes -
13060 '
13070 '     It is not possible  to  load  registers  directly  from
13080 ' BASIC.   Consequently,  a short machine language program is
13090 ' useful in order to load the proper registers, then execute a
13100 ' call to $RAMDIR.  This allows  the  parameters  to  take  on
13110 ' different  values  for  different  problems.   By having the
13120 ' luxury of being able to change parameters we have been  able
```

```
13130 ' to make the location of the directory buffer vary, depending
13140 ' on   what   other   machine language programs might be needed by
13150 ' the user.
13160 '
13170 FOR I=1 TO 16
   : READ RT(I)
   : NEXT I
13180 RETURN
13190 '
13200 DATA 217            :'EXX              ;SAVE REGISTERS
13210 DATA 33,0,0         :'LD HL,BUFFER     ;LOAD BUFFER ADDRESS
13220 DATA 6,0            :'LD B,DRIVE       ;LOAD DRIVE NUMBER
13230 DATA 14,0           :'LD C,FUNCT       ;LOAD DIRECTORY FUNCT
13240 DATA 205,0,0        :'CALL $RAMDIR     ;CALL $RAMDIR
13250 DATA 34,0,0         :'LD (ADDR),HL     ;LOAD START ADD OF DIR
13260 DATA 217            :'EXX              ;EXCHANGE REGISTERS
13270 DATA 201            :'RET              ;RETURN
13280 '
14000 '     Subroutine - Load Buffer Initialization M/L Routine
14010 '
14020 ' Purpose - To load the buffer Initialization machine language
14030 '     routine into the V(i) array.
14040 '
```

==

```
14050 ' Notes -
14060 '
14070 '      The data in the DATA statements  below  constitute  the
14080 ' actual   machine   language  routine  which  initializes  the
14090 ' directory buffer to zeroes.  The  buffer  address  locations
14100 ' must  be  initialized  prior  to  calling the routine.  That
14110 ' chore is accomplished in the BASIC  subroutine,  "INITIALIZE
14120 ' BUFFER."
14130 '
14140 FOR I=1 TO 16
   : READ V(I)
   : NEXT I
14150 RETURN
14160 '
14170 ' Machine Language Code for Initialization Routine
14180 '
14190 DATA 217        :'EXX                  ;SAVE REGISTERS
14200 DATA 33,0,0     :'LD    HL,BUFFER      ;FIRST LOCATION
14210 DATA 17,0,0     :'LD    DE,BUFFER+1    ;NEXT LOCATION
14220 DATA 1,255,9    :'LD    BC,0A00H       ;BUFFER LENGTH
14230 DATA 54,0       :'LD    (HL),00H       ;STORE 1ST ZERO
14240 DATA 237,176    :'LDIR                 ;FILL BUFFER
14250 DATA 217        :'EXX                  ;EXCHANGE REGISTERS
14260 DATA 201        :'RET                  ;RETURN
14270 '
```

for heavy commercial and industrial use, are at the high end of the price continuum for the base systems ($5000 to $7000 plus). All are Z80-based systems and run CP/M. Cromemco also produces a derivitive of CP/M called CDOS as well as a UNIX-like DOS (produced originally by Bell Labs and used on minicomputers) called CROMIX.

Osborne 1.   Another entry to the microcomputer market for late 1981 was the Osborne 1. Although it has not been on the market long enough to prove itself, it may provide an interesting alternative for some work station situations. The Osborne is a Z80-based system like many of the others. It is packaged in a portable configuration and comes complete with an impressive amount of software including CP/M, WORDSTAR, SUPERCALC, MBASIC, and CBASIC. All this came for a total price of $1795, which included a number of standard interfaces. By late 1981 a barely adequate communications program, MicroLink by Wordcraft, was available. The primary disadvantage of the Osborne when first distributed were the disk drives, which were single-density units. Double-density conversion later became available.

Digital Equipment Corporation (DEC).   In mid-1982 Digital Equipment Corporation (DEC), which had, to that time, stayed out of the microcomputer business, announced an impressive family of microcomputers in May, 1982. The series included the Rainbow (PC100), DECmate II (PC200), and the Professional (PC325 and PC350). The Rainbow, incorporating both a Z80 8-bit cpu and an 8088 16-bit cpu, was obviously designed to compete head-on with IBM's personal computer. The Rainbow, operating under either (or both) CP/M 80 and CP/M 86 (the eight and sixteen bit versions of CP/M) is also able to read diskettes generated by the IBM PC. At a list price considerably below IBM's it was apparent that DEC intended to give IBM considerable competition. Priced at the time of announcement the Rainbow was priced at about $3400 competing with not only the IBM PC but also with the Apple III (and fully configured Apple II) as well as the TRS-80 Model II. The standard configuration contains 64K bytes of memory expandable to 256K bytes.

The DECmate II, an extension of the DECmate I word processor, was designed primarily for word processing and uses DEC's 6120 16-bit cpu. The DECmate II is configured with 64K words (sixteen bits) of memory capable of expansion. A Z80 option is available, partly to allow the running of CP/M on the system. Without doubt, however, the two Professionals are top-of-the-line with the 325 originally priced at about $4000 and the 350 at about $5000. The Professional was configured with an F11 cpu (PDP-11/23, a 16-bit processor), 256K bytes of memory expandable to one megabyte, as well as other features. The systems use an operating system which is a subset of one of DEC's standard operating systems used on the PDP11 series and supports file structures consistent with the VAX series minicomputers. The market obviously targeted by Digital is the large corporate enterprise.

COST/PERFORMANCE CONSIDERATIONS

The foregoing review of hardware was not designed to be comprehensive. It unlikely that a complete list could be assembled that would not be out of date by the time it was published. Those mentioned are listed either because of their market positions or the aggressiveness with which they are being marketed. When looking for microcomputers for manager's work stations (or for other purposes) it is important to consider all the hardware and software factors mentioned so far. Some machines should not be considered for the work station concept: the Apple II, the Commodore PET, and various machines designed primarily for home use such as the ATARI.

Without question the best price/performance/investment ratio can be produced by either the TRS-80 Model III or the Osborne 1. They both have their deficiencies, however, and for large-scale users of microcomputers considerations other than the base cost can be important. For about $4000, including all hardware and software, a work station can be structured for either system. This is the price where the cost of the computer hardware (not including printers or modems) begins with virtually all other systems. Consequently, with any of the other systems we must expect a total cost of $5000 to $7000 and, depending on the software selection, could easily spend $10,000. As noted, however, if the deficiencies of these systems do not cause hardship, then the TRS-80 Model III and the Osborne constitute excellent hardware/software alternatives. Some of the newer systems, such as IBM's, undoubtedly will become major contenders by the mid 1980s but it is unlikely that all the software will be available before that time.

Remember, the key issue in acquiring a microcomputer is software availability for immediate, productive use. The second consideration then becomes the hardware on which the software can run. If an excessive amount of original programming is required, it could run up the cost of micro acquisitions considerably. But other factors also can be important, availability of quick and reliable service when a machine breaks down (and it will), vendor support, and many of the areas already discussed in this book. The point is, a manager's work station can be structured today (largely with off-the-shelf software) that can make large numbers of white-collar managers more productive and allow them to use their time and staff more productively. The purpose of this chapter has been to demonstrate how a manager's work station can be structured today, not to promote particular products.

One of the primary problems that becomes quickly apparent when considering microcomputer hardware and software is the large number of new products constantly entering the marketplace. In fact, by the late 1980s it is quite possible that manufacturers like DEC (Digital Equipment Corporation) will have reduced relatively large time-sharing systems to desktop size. These and other problems and opportunities involved in planning for microcomputers in large organizations will be addressed in Chapter 5.

5

Planning
for Microcomputers

Large organizations are frequently "penny wise and pound foolish," but never is this more obvious than when those institutions deal with computer technology. A primary reason for such short-sightedness is the fact that computer installations typically require larger expenditures than is usual for many other departments. These expenditures cannot be easily charged back to the consuming public, whether clients, customers, students, or citizens. Consequently, managers are often confronted with authorizing large sums of money for a technology they only barely comprehend. This ignorance of computing is often coupled with inadequate planning for the deployment of new technologies as they become available. As microcomputers became widespread in the late 1970s some of the organizational problems inherent in large establishments affected their acquisition.

Computing in general has suffered as well the deployment of microcomputers. Because the problems are general in character, so are at least some of the solutions. One of the problems in dealing with computer technology is the rate of growth and change in the technology itself. As already noted, however, it is possible to forecast the rate of change sufficiently well so that short and medium range planning can be done. The planning issue, in turn, reduces to relatively standard systems analysis.

Chapter 1 noted that the failure to plan for the use of microcomputers results in poor deployment rather than none at all, because large organizations are acquiring microcomputers, with or without planning. The lack of planning simply means that a major technology for the improvement of productivity of white-collar workers is poorly used and probably ends up costing far more than is necessary. Waste, duplication, and inefficiency lead inescapably to more costly modes of organizational behavior than does responsible planning.

By the early 1980s more variety in computing hardware and software was available than ever before, and this led to considerable confusion. It was apparent by the late 1970s that computing was moving away from batch processing to online, interactive systems for all manner of tasks. A planning time-line should stipulate what the distribution is now between batch processing and interactive processing, what it is likely to be one year from now, and what it should be five years from now. Interactive computing itself then can be subdivided by determining what should be the share processed by smaller, decentralized (or distributed) systems. This chapter attempts to address the second issue: planning for micros and how to accomplish it. During the 1980s microcomputers will play a major role in the data processing needs of large organizations. Even by early 1982 estimates suggested that as much as 90 percent of all micros were sold for business purposes and that a significantly large proportion went to large organizations.

The planning process implies that several things have happened in the organization. First, planning necessitates a clear understanding of the problems involved. Second, it requires that some institutional policies and goals be established (concerning computing and microcomputing) which meet the needs of the organization. And third, it involves the elaboration of appropriate procedures for implementing the policies and solving the problems.

PROBLEMS IN THE DEPLOYMENT OF MICROCOMPUTERS

The primary problems facing the organizational planner in dealing with microcomputers can be listed rather easily. They deal with selection, installation, maintenance, integration, training, and support. Issues of selection include hardware, software, and the organizational level that makes the decisions. The other problems not only involve the fixing of organizational responsibility, but also require some substantive decisions concerning who (what department) has these responsibilities and what the intensity or level of involvement should be. Just as IBM reorganized itself in 1981 in a vertical manner across all its product lines from typewriters to large mainframe computers, so most large organizations should provide a comprehensive vertical approach to information-processing solutions. This is particularly important in a technological environment in which virtually all devices from typewriters (or at least their successors) to mainframes are likely to be part of large distributed networks by the early 1990s.

Selection of Microcomputers

Focus on Software.   Too frequently decision-makers have tended to focus on the hardware available rather than on the functions to be performed by it. The first step in dealing with computing in general, and interactive computing more particularly, is to identify what functions are to be performed and how they can be accomplished most efficiently and effectively. Microcomputers can find a place in almost all computing environments.

Some problems, of course, required computing resources beyond the capabilities of the microcomputers available in the early 1980s, especially those needing large data files or very large memories. As the distinctions among microcomputers, minicomputers, and mainframe computers become increasingly blurred with improvements in technology, there will be fewer problems that cannot be solved by computers. Sometimes, however, there can be cooperation between large and small computers, with the small ones handling problems at the beginning or the end of the process while the large ones provide intermediate, large-scale processing. This implies that micros should be provided with communications facilities with access to centralized resources.

As noted in Chapter 3 there are a large number of problems that can be easily and effectively accommodated with small computers. And as the use of the 16-bit machines becomes more widespread in the mid-1980s the areas of use will increase dramatically. Indeed, by the early 1990s the cost/performance characteristics of 32-bit processors should allow "microcomputers" the size of typewriters (or smaller) to have the processing power and memory sizes of the largest computers of the late 1970s. But what is implied by all of this is that when deploying any computer system (and particularly a microcomputer), we should first be concerned with the availability of software to accomplish the computing needed and then seek hardware on which to run the software.

The issue of software is closely related to the problem of how much support is required for the systems acquired. Software not available "off-the-shelf" will have to written. Even when we have been impressed by a polished demonstration of a newly marketed microcomputer, we must recognize that it takes from 12 to 18 months for the primary manufacturer of the system and auxiliary supporting vendors to provide a wide range of software after the introduction of a device. It is likely that Radio Shack or IBM would disagree with this estimate, but we have only to look at the track records of several vendors. Fifteen months after the introduction of the TRS-80 Model III, Radio Shack and others did not have even previously existing Model I software ready to run on the Model III. Six months after the introduction of the IBM personal computer in 1981 it was still not possible to recommend immediate acquisition of this unit for use as a manager's work station simply because of the unavailability of software. Apple's Model III was still not selling well two years after its first introduction because of a lack of software. And Osborne's CP/M-based system continued to have a dearth of software six to nine months after its introduction simply because CP/M, while widespread in its use, was still not universal in the way it is implemented on various syustems even if that means just being able to acquire software on the correctly sized diskette recorded in a compatible manner. (It takes time to get the software ready and in use.)

Implications for Hardware. Once we have identified the range of software that meets the potential uses for microcomputers, we then can proceed to evaluate hardware. First and foremost, it will not help to wait another six months, nor will a search extended over a year be very helpful. The reason for this is that the technology is developing so rapidly that new products will be available even before our search is completed. Consequently, a long, drawn-out evaluation procedure will never catch up with the changing technology (at least not during the 1980s). Any acquisition today is doomed to be somewhat obsolete by tomorrow. This fact underscores the importance of making acquisition decisions on the basis of software availability rather than on what is the latest in hardware technology. If the two happen to come together, fine, but if they do not, then software should be the deciding factor.

However, there are some criteria for hardware selection that might prove useful. After determining the immediate availability of software, we must address the problem of memory capacity, disk capacity, and access to special-purpose hardware for unique or unusual functions (voice input/output, graphics, color, and so forth). If memory is too restrictive or disk capacity is too small or auxilliary devices are unavailable, then we should look further. Hardware enhancements need not, however, come from the primary computer manufacturer. There are large numbers of hardware enhancements available for Apples, TRS-80s, and S-100 microcomputers from independent manufacturers, and the same undoubtedly will be the case for IBM personal computers and others that gain wide-spread popularity. This issue itself introduces problems of acquisition, simply because it takes time and effort to track down all the hardware that might be necessary or desirable.

Even when all software and hardware enhancements can be acquired, additional criteria should be considered. Because the primary means of access will be through a keyboard, that keyboard should have good tactile qualities. The display screen should be restful and easy to watch. The physical design of the equipment should blend well with other office decor. Switches should be easily accessible without physically moving the equipment to use them. It should be possible to access cable connectors, yet at the same time keep cables out of the way when the equipment is in use. An appropriate (synchronous or asynchronous) communications interface should be available. All these factors, and perhaps others, can be important in ensuring that the equipment will be used as intended rather than simply gathering dust on a shelf. What has been said of the microcomputer itself is also true of its peripherals: printers, disks, and other items. Once appropriate software has been identified (functionally rather than by brand name) and a micro has been found with the software and physical characteristics desired, acquisition can then take place, providing that other factors (yet to be discussed) are also understood and confronted.

Installing the Equipment

For those of us with experience in the use of microcomputers the concept of installation may seem trivial. Because most micros simply come in one or more boxes with the purchaser being expected to set up the equipment, installation can be a problem. Some retail vendors of microcomputers will deliver and set up the system for an organization; others will not. Most of the people who are the end users of micros in an office do not know how to set up the machines. Consequently, some internal agency within the organization must assume the responsibility for installation and testing of any acquisition. In some cases "installation" may extend to dealing with the local telephone or cable television company to ensure that a line, equipped with the proper connectors, is installed. If micros are to be used appropriately within an organization, it is essential to provide services such as installation so that the end user will feel comfortable in the use of the system.

Installation means not only the installation of the hardware, but also the appropriate installation of any standard software. For a manager's work station this involves organizing one or more diskettes to include the operating system along with any supplementary programs to be used on a regular basis. It also may mean that files of commands for automatic submission of job streams be structured and put in place. In large computer installations these tasks are frequently the responsibility of the systems programming group, but for microcomputers, who is to take responsibility? If a central computing center is delegated that responsibility, then it will have to designate one or more individuals within the computing center to handle these tasks. Such an individual would need training in micro hardware and software so that the tasks could be accomplished with ease and dispatch. A large organization should develop a policy to deal with fixing the responsibilities for installation.

Maintaining the System

Although microcomputers are generally reliable items of hardware, sooner or later something will break down and need fixing. In a broad sense, maintenance may be required for both hardware and software. At this point we are concerned with hardware support—software support will be addressed later. There are several ways in which a large organization can attack the problem of hardware maintenance: (1) on a time and materials basis (2) with a maintenance contract with either the primary vendor or an independent vendor or (3) through an internal maintenance unit. The problems inherent in providing maintenance for microcomputers are much the same as for terminals.

If the number of machines is not too great, a time and materials system, possibly requiring the return of the hardware to the vendor, would be appropriate. This approach may be adequate if time is not a problem—that is, if the organization can afford to have one or more machines out of service for several days. This approach, combined with having some spare machines, is probably the least expensive maintenance alternative. If time is somewhat critical, and the organization possesses a moderate number of instruments, then an on-site maintenance agreement is likely appropriate. By "moderate" is meant some number less than about 80 machines. Depending on the vendor of maintenance services, maintenance contracts could range from $20 per month to $50 or more per machine. If we assume that the average cost is about $30 monthly, then the cost of maintenance contracts for 80 machines would be the approximate equivalent of the salary necessary for a technician. Frequently, however, even if the number of machines is considerably fewer than 80, the cost of maintenance contracts provide a sufficiently major percentage of a salary, when combined with other functions (maintenance of terminals, for example), to make the hiring of a technician a viable alternative. The ultimate decision on this issue, of course, is one of economy: For a given situation, what is the most cost-effective method for providing reliable maintenance for the equipment?

An Integrated System
of Microcomputers

One of the primary objectives in planning for microcomputing in a large organization is to provide an integrated system. "Integrated" in this sense has two meanings. First, there should be sufficient standardization of software and hardware to provide for beneficial purchase agreements and discounts from vendors. Second, any acquisition of micros should be integrated into the overall computing plan for the organization regardless of whether this implies hardware integration through networking or an understanding of the information-processing role played by the micros. Actually there is a third way for us to understand the term "integration", although this is discussed elsewhere in detail: providing an integrated hardware/software system friendly to the end user. For present purposes we shall confine the discussion to the first two forms of integration.

Standardization.   Standardization of software and hardware can have a number of beneficial results, although such commonality is not easily achieved. When hardware and software is standardized it allows a large organization to purchase in quantity. When purchases in quantity are made, it almost always is possible to negotiate beneficial discounts, thus making acquisitions of microcomputers even more attractive economically. With almost any hardware vendor it is possible to obtain a discount of from about 10 to 20 percent on purchases. This means that for a fixed budget it is frequently possible to buy additional equipment within budgetary constraints or with a flexible budget to acquire equipment with the lowest possible budgetary implications. Standardization (or the lack thereof) also can help determine the level of support (programming, maintenance, etc.) made available to the end user or can influence the cost of such support. Certainly the cost of maintenance contracts will be lower if standardization is the rule rather than the exception.

Micros and Information Processing.   If there is no function that can be served by microcomputers in a large organization, then they should not be acquired. It is part of the purpose of this book, however, to demonstrate the role micros can play in an overall plan of information processing for a large organization. While an individual may acquire objects for their own sake, organizations normally should make acquisitions only for the pursuit of specifically defined objectives. Consequently, when the decision is made to acquire micros on a large scale, that decision should be made with some explicit understanding concerning the manner in which the equipment will contribute to the overall information-processing needs of that organization. This assumes (perhaps incorrectly) that the organization already has some general computing plan in place and is actually operating on the basis of that plan. Typically, however, people in large organizations talk a good deal about plans, write large numbers of memos about plans and actually produce documents called plans but fail to develop these plans. In any event, especially if the microcomputer is to become part of a distributed data processing system, it is essential that somebody within the organization address the way in which micros are to be integrated into the overall solution for data processing.

Forces Against Integration.   It is relatively easy to make positive statements regarding integration; it is even easy to get verbal agreement by large numbers of people to the general objectives expressed. It is extremely difficult, however, to get either individuals or institutions to behave as if the concept of hardware/software integration extended beyond mere words. The reasons for this situation are numerous. Especially with microcomputers, people tend to become strong, vociferous champions of systems they may own or with which they have had experience. Therefore, a position of advocacy for this or that machine tends to develop regardless of whether a particular product is appropriate for the use at hand. The problem of integration becomes exacerbated by such advocacy and may, in the end, prohibit any form of standardization. This phenomenon is particularly virile on college and university campuses but probably exists in virtually all large organizations. All of us, after all, like the familiar and distrust the different.

Organizationally, another factor inhibiting integration is one of the points mentioned in Chapter 1: either distrust of the central computing facility or excessive and misplaced feelings of departmental autonomy. If budgeting is decentralized, it then may be next to impossible to achieve appropriate levels of integration. The failure to provide integration will lead to inadequate and inappropriate uses of microcomputers (and other resources for that matter). A caveat is in order: We need not identify the attempt to integrate with monolithic control. There are good reasons in any large organization to provide more than one alternative for solving information processing needs. There are compelling reasons, however, to make the attempt to prevent anarchy, and some of these reasons have just been stated. Others will be mentioned as we proceed.

Training Demands

Before any large-scale deployment of microcomputers takes place, provisions should be made for training institutional personnel in their use and value. There are at least three specific training needs in a large organization, depending on the functions of the individuals involved. First, of course, is the need to provide some training for the end users—the target audience for micros. Such training must include hardware use and more specifically, the use of selected software. Within the context of the manager's work station, it would be necessary to train various people to use the word processor, the communications program, the planning program, and any other systems that are not entirely self-evident. Training can take at least two forms. Classical classroom training can be given, and most large organizations are prepared to provide such training in one fashion or another. The training may be developed internally, may be contracted with an outside consultant, or may be supplied by the hardware or software vendor(s). And the micros themselves can be used along with computer-assisted instruction modules as training devices.

Second, a somewhat different—and more specialized—kind of training is needed for those people called systems analysts and usually attached to central data processing units. The function of the systems analyst is to evaluate a request for data processing services and to suggest the appropriate way to meet the need. The difficulty is that most systems analysts are trained to provide solutions in terms of large mainframe computing systems. In a period of rapidly changing technology the objective should be to recommend the best, most cost-effective solutions to data processing needs, problems, and opportunities, not solutions limited to the use of particular forms of computing. If an institutional policy is established to make extensive use of microcomputers, therefore, it becomes not only important but absolutely essential that those people who provide the systems analytic functions be trained (or retrained) to make appropriate recommendations to include the new hardware capabilities. This level of training is considerably more technical in character than the training of end users, and it will be a level of training much more difficult to provide. The most likely sources for people who can do such training are management consultant firms, although many large organizations have staff internally (perhaps not even connected with the DP operations) capable of providing training. Consequently, when a search is made for training personnel it should be internal as well as external.

The third level of training is even more technical than that implied for systems analysts. A few people within the organization have to be trained to assist with detailed hardware and software support. Such training may be acquired from some vendors but is more likely to come from the same sources suggested for systems analysts. The number of people within a large organization requiring this level of training may be quite small, but the need is real if large numbers of micros are acquired. Training topics might include something on microcomputer hardware, the internals of the operating system(s) used on the micros, and something about primary software used across the organization. This issue relates back to the entire problem of maintenance as well as to the level of support any organizational policy might dictate. If a comprehensive training program is ignored, then it is almost guaranteed that micros will be poorly and inadequately used.

Levels of Support

The crux of what has been said concerning selection, installation, maintenance, integration, and training ultimately comes down to a policy decision on the level of support to be provided for the use of microcomputers. It may range from the minimal to the extensive. If the policy is made (and implemented) to support micros extensively, then they are apt to be used well. On the other hand, if either consciously or by default the decision is made to provide little or no support, then micros will not be used to the fullest extent. Any decision concerning the level of support will have an economic impact. The more extensive the support, the more costly the overall plan for micros in an organization—but this is true of any technology.

An overall plan for microcomputing can include incremental expansion of support simply because, if only a few micros are acquired, the level of support can be quite different from a situation in which hundreds or even thousands of machines are purchased. It also is possible that various support functions need not all be implemented concurrently but may be implemented incrementally. The point is, it will not be possible to make coherent decisions concerning the other problems discussed until the issue of support (including both its distribution and extent) is addressed. Ultimately, when organizations do acquire large numbers of micros, they will tend to support them, even in the absence of explicit policy. This issue, like many of the others we have noted, can be done well (in a cost-effective and efficient manner), or it can be done badly (with significant loss of time, effort, and money).

ORGANIZATIONAL POLICIES AND GOALS

Throughout this book the implicit argument has been that there is a close relationship among three major conponents in an organization: data processing (including management information systems), telecommunications, and office administration (focusing on a technology called the "manager's work station"). In universities, corporations, and government these three components often are separated by quite wide distances, organizationally, and sometimes physically. In large universities, for example, it is common for the telecommunications function to be placed under the physical plant administrator, who has little communication with the data processing people.

Yet decisions concerning telephone systems and other internal communications can greatly influence the ability of data processing to deliver computing services. At worst this situation can mean establishing separate (and not necessarily equal) communications systems competing for space on the same facilities (poles, conduits, etc.). Office administrators — in any organization — are often even more removed from telecommunications and data processing decisions and may end up attempting to automate without any thought to the way in which office automation should be merged with the other two functions.

Sometimes upper level managers simply throw up their hands in despair as a result of these organizational issues. As J. H. Morgan has observed (*Telecommunications*, January 1982, p. 53), some upper level managers will simply choose among the least objectionable, commenting:

DP will take a job and maybe, three months later, we'll get some output — all wrong.

Telecommunication people are never around when you need them, and they hide from advanced telecommunications which involve voice, data, and video.

Office administrators would just as soon sit around in green eye shades and pretend that technology doesn't exist.

In light of these attitudes Morgan states that the unit most likely to take over office automation in the long run will be the one which learns about the others first. Whichever unit becomes the leader in office automation must have an appreciation of the other two. Morgan suggests that the ratio of leadership in office automation, across the country, will be about 40 percent from DP/MIS, 40 percent from office administration, and 20 percent from telecommunications.

In any event, what was noted above concerning the more general problem of office automation is equally true of microcomputer deployment. The primary uses of micros during the 1980s will be as the basis for automated offices of the next decade. The result is that micros may come to organizations by way of office administration through systems like Xerox's Ethernet or Wang's distributed networks. If large organizations persistently fail to implement an appropriate policy for the deployment and acquisition of not only microcomputers but also other forms of office automation, it is likely that deployment will take place with all the attendant problems outlined above. We noted earlier that the strategy being pursued in IBM is an integrated approach to all these issues and they, implicitly, are sponsoring data processing as the appropriate center for concerted action.

As a matter of fact, this is a good perspective.

While it is not possible to solve all of the organizational problems inherent in planning for microcomputers and office automation, it is possible to provide an outline of the issues that should be faced by such a plan and to suggest what some of the responses might be. Not all of the uses of micros are involved with office automation, although, thus far, we have tended to focus on the potentials of microcomputers within the administrative and managerial context For the most part, a micro policy should address the following issues:

1. *The Deployment of Microcomputers.* The needs for which microcomputers might provide some respite should be identified. Some of these needs have been listed elsewhere in this book. They include use in an office as intelligent work stations, as training devices, as control devices and, in general, whenever a modicum of machine intelligence is needed apart from any mainframe computer system.

2. *The Role of the Data Processing Center.* In order to insure that the organization provides a means for the orderly acquisition of microcomputers and that they avoid the problems identified earlier in this chapter, it is likely that the responsibility for micros should be placed in the hands of an existing data processing system with overlapping responsibilities. Consistent with this point is the premise that whomever acquires the responsibility for managing the deployment of micros, there must be established an appropriate support staff. In particular, the responsible agency should do the following:

    a. Provide some level of software support consistent with the aims and goals of the organization.

    b. Provide some level of hardware support which would include:
        i. Organization of maintenance agreements covering any microcomputers acquired.
        ii. Assistance in the writing of specifications for microcomputers for whatever purposes the micros are being acquired.

    c. Ensure that all acquisitions fall within the boundaries of an overall plan for computing in the organization, particularly with respect to purposes for which the micro(s) is/are to be acquired. This should include at least:
        i. Integration of any micros into the communications systems by which computing services are delivered.
        ii. Minimization of proliferation of different hardware systems and inconsistent operating systems.

3. *Design Responsibilities.* If the objective of data processing is to solve organizational problems, the solutions should be those that are most cost-effective and technologically effficient. It should be the responsibility of the computing center, data processing center, or other agency overseeing microcomputing to provide competent advice and counsel concerning the uses of micros. As the capabilities of micros increase, more and more applications thought to be only within the sphere of a central computing system will be distributed out to end users—or at least will be closer to end users. This does not mean the end user will need a lower or inferior level of support, just that the support is likely to be somewhat different than what it traditionally has been.

4. *The Limits of Central Responsibility.* Just as the organizational policy should address the specific responsibilities for deploying microcomputers, it also should spell out the limits to those responsibilities. Can a department desiring micros actually use them as intended? If so, then acquisition of and payment for the machines should be a concern of normal budgeting processes, not of the data processing department. In other words, the data processing division ordinarily should not become another purchasing agent or department, nor should it make judgments on the budgetary implications of purchases. In any event, the policy should define the limitations of authority.

IMPLEMENTING THE POLICIES

In order for any policies to be effective there must be some method established for implementation. These constitute the procedures to be followed when the policy demands are carried out. When it comes to the planning, acquisition, and uses of microcomputers there are a number of organizational units that must be involved. Without enforcement of a microcomputer policy, the proliferation and waste discussed earlier will be rampant. The bottom line in any large organization as to whether an acquisition policy will be enforced is whether the purchasing department maintains procedures that trap acquisitions and requires that some sign-off document be appended to the purchase order. In small organizations this may not be so important, but any organization that has centralized purchasing procedures must have the cooperation of the purchasing department.

If the central computing facility is to be the general overseer for microcomputer acquisitions, once a request for a micro is referred to it, then an appropriate person within that unit must be delegated the authority to deal with the request. If the request comes from a systems analyst who has determined that the most cost-effective solution for some DP problem is the use of a micro, then the disposition may be perfunctory. A rubber-stamp approach to authorization also may be the case when dealing with an engineering department or with a computer science department in a university, simply because such units have applications that can be handled internally without involving any central computing facility personnel or service. In other words, when a user department has intenal expertise of its own, close supervision may be unnecessary, unless the potential use focuses on broader applications within the organization. Conversely, if a request has been made by a potential user who is relatively naive concerning computing, then greater supervision would be necessary and proper.

Regardless of the overseeing agency (and we shall assume it to be the central computing service), there is a short list of questions evey potential user should be required to answer. The following list certainly is not exhaustive and perhaps should be expanded to include items specific to particular organizations. In any event, potential microcomputer users should be prepared to answer them.

1. What is the purpose of the acquisition? The answer must contain a description of the proposed applications for the computer and should seek to answer an additional question: How is this solution better than using a central facility?

2. How does this acquisition fit into the overall planning of the organization for computing? "Computing" in this sense also might include word processing and office automation as well as more traditional forms of computing services.

3. Is acceptable software available for the proposed applications, or will software have to be written? If software is to be written, are funds and programmer time available? Will the central computing facility provide the programmers, or can outside contract programmers be acquired?

4. How will the microcomputer communicate with any central computing system if at all? Even though there may be no immediate plans for communication, sooner or later the user department making the acquisition will wish to communicate. Consequently, there must be some assurance that appropriate software is available (probably without programming a communications package) to support using the micro as a terminal. This consideration also includes stipulation of appropriate protocol (async or bisync).

5. Who will be responsible for installation of hardware and software? If installation will be the responsibility of the central computing center, then have the appropriate requests been placed?

6. Who is going to maintain the equipment? Is an on-site maintenance contract available? What are the maintenance costs?

7. Is training required to operate the system (both hardware and software)? If so, how is this training to be acquired?

If these questions (and others) cannot be adequately answered, then the user requesting the microcomputer probably should be sent back to reconsider the request. In particular, in order to effectively answer the first three items, it may be necessary to involve the people responsible for systems analysis in order to insure that such requests are appropriate within the context of the policies and procedures adopted by the organization.

The primary objective in these suggestions for policies and procedures is to protect both the end user and the central computing facility. The term "protect" taken in this context is understood to mean insuring the integrity of any data and information processed by either the central site or the local microcomputer. A term sometimes used in this context is "security." The point is, the central site is responsible for the integrity of organizational data and its security. The local user department often must use that data and may be able to make better use of it if there were local micros to assist. Uninformed use, however, often can lead to inappropriate use of the information and, at worst, can compromise its integrity. Even more to the point, if the micro does not accomplish the objectives of the local user department, it simply may be shelved to gather dust.

OPPORTUNITIES IN THE DEPLOYMENT OF MICROCOMPUTERS

Any organization that has taken into consideration the potential problems involved in the acquisition of microcomputers has before it many opportunities when the micros are properly deployed and used. In the most comprehensive sense, the widespread use of micros in large organizations will improve the productivity of white-collar workers and especially of management. A comprehensive microcomputing policy, depending on the level of networking and other conditions for integrated use within the organization, can go far in promoting the use of personal computers. Once deployed, however, the uses for micros include, but are not limited to, calculation or word processing or data communications.

Initially, people in central data processing sites may think of microcomputers as possibly degrading, or at least diluting, the central computing services. The fact of the matter is, however, that widespread use of micros is likely to encourage expanded central site activity as users become more familiar with the potential for computing. Moreover, for systems which really should be run on small computers rather than large ones, micros make dedicated applications possible that are accomplished at an appropriate level within the organization. This kind of computing, in turn, can reduce the demand on central computing and improve the response time of the large systems by eliminating large numbers of relatively (to the computer) trivial tasks. How can microcomputers be used effectively? We will take a look at how they have been used in large organizations in Chapter 6.

6

Case Studies
of Microcomputer Use

So far the uses of microcomputers in large organizations have been discussed in a somewhat abstract manner. That is because we have had little cause to demonstrate the use of micros in real organizations. In order to demonstrate how micros are being used, we will draw on some data from an industrial survey conducted in Dallas, Texas, in November 1981 and several case studies of actual implementations in real organizations. To make the presentation interesting and informative, it will not be a scientific treatise but rather will provide systematic examples of the uses of micros in real situations. If you have not already acquired a good idea of the ways in which micros can be used in almost any organization, this chapter should provide further insight. Remember: micros are here to stay. We can use the technology wisely and well, or we can use it poorly and inefficiently.

Part of the background work for this book included the development and administration of a short questionnaire in the fall of 1981. For purposes of simplicity (rather than of scientific sampling) the mailing list of the Dallas, Texas, chapter of the Data Processing Management Association was used as the population from which data was drawn. At that time the Dallas DPMA was one of the larger chapters in the country — and Dallas itself is one of the most volatile data processing markets. DPMA members are largely (though by no means exclusively) data processing middle-management personnel. Because of this specialized population, I anticipated some lack of information concerning microcomputing or even some resistance toward it. Both problems surfaced but in extremely small degree. In Chapter 2 it was noted that data processing managers are sometimes not the best sources of information on the uses of micros. We will see whether this has proven to be true in Dallas. Since the Dallas chapter sometimes contains more than one member from the same company, there is a little overlap in answers (although it turned out not to be very high). This means that any percentages are based on the number of individuals responding (136), rather than on the number of companies.

The decision of whether to use individual respondents or companies as the base for an analysis demonstrates a significant organizational issue in the deployment of micros. While it is true that in some mid-sized businesses (based on personnel estimates) a central office may have a grasp on the number of micros acquired and their uses, in very large organizations (such as Texas Instruments) the bureaucracy almost precludes that any single person or unit will know what is happening across the entire structure. This is a problem (or opportunity, depending on one's perspective) which frequently affects universities, large corporations, and governmental bodies.

The other source of information for this chapter was more detailed and in-depth data extracted in a case study format. At least one of the cases was acquired through correspondence with systems analyst, Carolyn Mark, at a production facility of a large Fortune 500 company (FMC Corporation, Bowling Green, Kentucky). This mid-south plant has access to very large-scale computing power through remote batch and on-line systems. A second case is taken from a published report and is an example of microcomputer use in a department of a large mid-western university: the Political Science Department of the University of Iowa (compare G. R. Boynton, "The Learning Process Continues", *Desktop Computing*, November 1981, pp. 58–60). This department was able to implement the use of micros not as teaching aids (the normal use in universities), but as work stations for the faculty. An attempt is made to integrate the case studies with the statistical data from Dallas in order to provide a clear description of the uses of microcomputers in actual use.

AN ORGANIZATIONAL OVERVIEW

Even an apparently simple question like defining a "large organization" turns out to be somewhat complicated. The term "large," in the context of this book, refers to both the size of the organization measured in number of employees and to the scale of computing power already used by the people in the organization. Consequently, we used both criteria here. Some companies—oil exploration companies are the among the best examples—employ relatively few people (often less than 100) but use one or more (usually more) very large computers (IBM 3033 class or larger). While there certainly is a relationship between size as measured only by employees and size measured by both people and computers, neither measurement alone addressed the objectives of this book. Perhaps a better measurement would have been something like total cash flow per year, but this number is difficult to acquire (with accuracy) and is not entirely comparable between the private and public sectors. In any event, the final definition of a "large organization" was one which employed 200 or more people or used large-scale on-site or remote computing. (Large-scale computing was defined as an IBM 4331 class machine or larger.)

Both of the institutions selected for presentation as case studies fell easily into the personnel size classification of "large," while one used large-scale on-site computing and the other used large-scale remote computing. Of the total number of people responding to the Dallas survey, 16.9 percent (23) worked in small organizations while 83.1 percent (113) worked in large organizations. This breakdown also is consistent with the organizational character and recruiting efforts of DPMA. Some other items were used in an effort to describe the organizations involved. For example, 50.8 percent of those responding to the survey worked in local subsidiaries of larger regional or national organizations while 49.2 percent worked in independent local organizations. This is probably consistent with the fact that Dallas has become a major national center of business and industry.

The median size of all organizations surveyed was 200. Of those responding, 51.5 percent indicated that the site at which they worked was not the only one owned by the organization in the metroplex (the entire Dallas/Ft. Worth area). The largest single number of people (25.4 percent) were from manufacturing concerns. Other categories included retail (3.2 percent), financial (8.7 percent), data processing (17.5 percent), government (2.4 percent), education (3.2 percent), miscellaneous other businesses (22.2 percent) and miscellaneous other organizations (17.5 percent). With respect to computing power, 74.4 percent used on-site large-scale computing and 30.8 percent used large-scale remote computing. The latter figures include some with both kinds of computing: 20.3 percent used both on-site and remote, 54.1 percent used only on-site, 10.5 percent used only remote, and 15.0 percent used neither. Those who used neither were classified as belonging to small organizations.

The overwhelming majority of both the on-site and remote computer users accessed at least some online systems. In fact only 9.6 percent of the on-site users and 5.9 percent of the remote users were still using batch-only computing, although the largest single percentages of both groups used both batch and online computing. Batch computing is not dead (and apparently is not even going away), but very large amounts of online computing are occurring. By way of contrast, about half as many people (in both computing groups) are using online computing as were using batch-only computing.

A PROFILE OF LARGE
ORGANIZATION MICRO USERS

In the Dallas survey more than half (54.4 percent) the entire group responding indicated their organizations possessed one or more microcomputers. In fact, across the entire group the median number of micros owned was 3.5 per organization, although I suspect few respondents really knew exactly how many personal computers were actually in use. Regardless of whether the organization was large or small, about the same proportion of respondents reported institutionally acquired micros: 52.2 percent for small organizations and 54.9 percent for large ones. These numbers included both those already using micros and those with explicit plans to acquire micros in either the current fiscal year or the next one. The latter two classes represented only a small proportion of the respondents in large organizations (5.6 percent).

Although the distributions are far from normal for either the number of micros in use or the actual number of employees, it is instructive to note that the median number of employees reported by respondents from small organizations was 12.0 and from large ones was 299.6 — a considerable difference. A marked difference also was noted in the number of micros in use: 1.25 for small organizations and 4.6 for large ones. If we use the mean, a greater difference occurs: 1.4 micros for small organizations, 49.4 for large ones. Because of the kind of sample we used and because a very few large organizations had a very large number of micros, the medians are probably better estimates of the actual average use.

The two organizations selected for closer scrutiny clearly were large. The Cable Crane and Excavator Division of FMC Corporation in Bowling Green, Kentucky, employs several hundred people and has a local data processing department of 12 people. That department, along with various user departments, operates remotely to dual IBM 3081s — a large-scale computing system. The large computing facility within FMC operates primarily as a utility, with programming and user services being provided locally. Much of the impetus for the use of micros came initially from engineering users.

At the University of Iowa a somewhat different situation exists. It was a user department (Political Science) which opted in favor of micros.

About half of the department's 30 full-time staff had used the university's large computers on a regular basis: the other half had not used computers at all. The University of Iowa, like many large public institutions of higher education, employs several thousand people. The objectives of the Political Science Department, like those at FMC, were similar in that they were designed to gain greater productivity from the staff.

USING MICROCOMPUTERS

The actual uses of microcomputers are quite varied. While large organizations use central mainframes for such purposes as accounting, small ones use micros for the same purpose. A statistical summary of the uses listed would be meaningless, but it is interesting and instructive to see the variety of uses. The list below is taken directly from the responses of the Dallas survey. The list is organized alphabetically, and no attempt is made to indicate the number of times a single item was noted. In Chapter 3 we did point out a number of potential uses of microcomputers and referred to the data from the Dallas survey. The list on which those comments were based follows:

Account inquiry
Auditing
Balance of accounts
Biomedical preventive maintenance
Budgeting
Control devices (for other systems)
Database inquiry system (limited)
Data collection
Data collection (at operating level)
Data collection (financial)
Data collection (intelligent data entry)
Data collection (laboratory control devices)
Data validation before batch submission
Dealer support
Distributed processing
Drilling reports (oil exploration)
Education
Education (computer-assisted instruction)
Education (data processing training)
Engineering
Engineering (analog to digital analysis)
Engineering (analysis and problem solving)
Finance (forecasting)
Finance (petty cash)
Financial analysis
Financial analysis (cash flow forecasting)
Financial analysis (profit planning)

Financial modeling (pro forma, etc.)
Financial modeling (using VISICALC)
Graphics
Hardware control (status of real-time systems)
Insurance proposals
Intelligent desk calculators
Intelligent terminals
Intelligent interface device
Inventory control
Manager's work station
Monitor for large CPU performance
Operations research
Organizational maintenance (organization charts, lists, etc.)
Personnel programs
Plotting
Point-of-sales
Policy ratings (automated)
Process control
Production control
Production planning models
Project control (time and cost estimates, etc.)
Purchase order status
Run costs history
Sales and marketing applications
Scheduling (staff)
Security control system (locks, badge validation, etc.)
Shipping records
Simulations
Software development
Statistics (actuarial benefits)
Statistics (departmental research)
Statistics (economic analysis)
Statistics (trend analysis)
Stock balance
Tax computations
Training (administrative systems)
Word processing

Each of these uses is consistent with the capabilities of microcomputers. And as micros become faster and contain more memory, other functions often reserved for large mainframes will be accomplished locally on the desk of the user, rather than at some central site. One of the primary purposes for which micros were acquired was for word processing, and many of the uses can be subsumed under the manager's work station concept.

Case Study One: FMC

In somewhat greater detail we can look at the experience of the two case study organizations, FMC and the University of Iowa.* As of late 1981 the

*Information concerning the use of microcomputers used by permission of appropriate FMC authorities.

FMC plant in Kentucky possessed nine micros, mostly TRS-80 Model IIs. The TRS-80s were all acquired primarily as word processors. In addition, one micro (a Numeric Micro machine) was being used to develop numerical control tapes for the various machines used in the plant. Attached to the Numeric Micro is a plotter and tape input/output device. The micro is used to develop the appropriate numerical control data, which is then saved to tape. The tape is reread by the micro, and the plotter is used to simulate at least some of the functions of the target machine.

In this particular case the plotter is attached through a two-way RS232 switch and is shifted back and forth between the Numeric Micro machine and TRS-80 Model I. The Model I is frequently used as a terminal to the central mainframe, particularly by engineers using large-scale graphics software such as the SAS/Graph (a subsystem of Statistical Analysis System), which runs on large IBM machines. The plotter, incidentally, is from Hewlett Packard. The use of these two micros on the plant floor also has led to the use of the Numeric Micro as a scheduling machine for process control of the various machines there.

The area of production control, as might be expected in a manufacturing plant, has received considerable attention. The TRS-80 Model IIs, in addition to being used as word processors in the office, also are used to assist in shop maintenance. It was once very confusing for the staff to maintain an adequate schedule for routine maintenance of the machinery. A relatively simple program was written (by the maintenance department) to read a data file and output a lubrication schedule for each machine each week. The input data are taken from the maintenance books for each machine. Some of the heavy equipment needs weekly maintenance, while other equipment needs lubrication only quarterly. A consistent lubrication schedule is maintained through the use of the micros. A maintenance log also is kept on each machine (by the TRS-80 Model II) to record what is done when, and by whom, as well as other relevant data. The log, once its utility had been demonstrated, was moved to the mainframe computer, primarily as a by-product of the file size.

One of the more innovative uses of the TRS-80 concerns personnel issues. As with many large organizations, some employees felt that there were problems with promotions and the potential for upward mobility. As the staff in any organization stablizes, a tendency toward mobility stagnation occurs. If turnover is low, then opportunities for advancement will decrease; if turnover is high, then opportunities will abound, but the efficiency of the organization may decline. The local FMC management addressed this problem by posting all openings and encouraging applications from within.

In order to respond to potentially heavy responses (40 or more internal applications per opening are not unusual), an automated scoring system using the microcomputers was developed. A file is developed for each open position which includes data for each applicant. The applicant data consists of ratings by various people including the current supervisor, the potential supervisor, the Personnel Department, and any employee of the candidate's choice. The ratings are summarized and combined into a single score. These scores then are used in the screening of applicants. Each position is kept on a separate diskette, and rating are entered "online" at the several locations where TRS-80s are located.

Micros have proven useful in a miscellany of other applications at FMC. The Engineering Department has found them useful enough, and the engineers have learned BASIC well enough to do their own programming. This is illustrative of what is happening in several areas: Departments are being provided with micros on the assumption that their own personnel will do much of the programming, although programming services are available from the Data Processing Department. The TRS-80s are used by various departments to prepare regular status reports, and at least one programmer is using a machine as a development tool. Employee recreational programs are partially scheduled through the use of the micros as well.

Case Study Two:
University of Iowa

The situation in the Political Science Department at the University of Iowa is considerably different than that at FMC. First, there are fewer different uses of the micros than at FMC, although the number of micros purchased is larger. The two institutions have one primary objective in common: use of micros as word processors. At both Iowa and FMC there is full support given by the respective data processing departments, although the initial impetus for acquiring micros came from user departments. The broader objective in obtaining the micros was much the same at both FMC and at the university: to improve productivity. In the case of the Political Science Department, however, the decision was made to place a micro on the desk of all 30 full-time staff members. This included 20 faculty members, 5 secretaries, and 5 research and educational support people. Only the secretarial staff had printers.

The basic problem was how to improve the productivity of everyone in an environment where the major products are written research reports (articles, books, etc.). The teachers are prolific writers, and this accounts for the secretarial and research support staff. The computers purchased are Commodore CBM 8032s. Interestingly enough, they are tape-oriented rather than disk, perhaps a cost-saving decision. The word processing program is a simple one. As a faculty member completes a manuscript (or part thereof), he/she takes the resulting tape to the secretarial staff. The secretary prints the document, makes any appropriate corrections, and furnishes a proof copy to the faculty member.

Each of the micros is equipped with an RS232 interface, appropriate software, and a modem for use as a terminal to the central system. Communications are an important use of the micros. By using the central computing facility's electronic mail system, intradepartmental paper memoranda has decreased, with most communication taking place through the computer-based mail system. In late 1981 plans were being made for expanding micro use through new applications.*

Later in this chapter we will note some of the problems in implementation faced at both FMC and Iowa. Suffice it to say, however, that in both organizations the people that use the micros apparently have concluded that the experiments were a success and that the micros have improved productivity. Certainly selected tasks have been made easier for those using the micros. Although there is a feeling in both academic institutions and in business that the two types of organizations are quite different, the fact is that people in both organizations, and the management of both organizations are interested in greater productivity as well as worker satisfaction. Both of the units selected for more intensive study seem to suggest that these objectives were met.

PLANNING FOR MICROCOMPUTERS

The word "planning," at least when it involves computing, implies at least two things. First, it means an implementation plan for machines already ordered or on the verge of being ordered or, in the words of Rocky Smolin, "What to do until the computer comes" (*Interface Age*, March 1982, pp. 75–79). Second, it means a futures-oriented outlook that perceives the importance of planning for the uses of new and helpful technology. With respect to the first, we can offer only some general observations; and with respect to the latter, it appears that nearly everyone is doing a poor job. One respondent in the Dallas survey reported there was a management philosophy that mitigated against the use of micros, although that same person reported that some micros were in use in her organization. This particular situation was indicative of the position taken by another respondent, who suggested that the acquisition of micros happens "with or without any planning."

Generally, of the Dallas respondents working for large organizations that had some micros, 45.5 percent (25) reported absolutely no plans for further use; 52.7 percent (29) reported informal and unfocused plans; and only (1.8 percent (1) reported a systematic corporate policy for implementing the use of micros. At the University of Iowa's Political Science Department the impetus came not from institutional planning but from the inter-

*G. R. Boynton, "The Learning Process Continues," *Desktop Computing*, November 1981, pp. 58–60.

est and leadership exercised by the department's chairperson. At the FMC plant in Kentucky micros were introduced in an informal manner. The point is, future planning is minimal and apparently is not taken very seriously by any organization. The situation is even worse with groups that do not already have microcomputers. Of these agencies, only nine reported even informal plans for future deployment.

Just as future planning is not being done well, so implementation planning is not being accomplished with any great dispatch. As Smolin pointed out, there is some implementation planning that should take place before the delivery of microcomputers. Prior to placing any orders, of course, some analysis should be done concerning the potential uses of the machines. Provision must be made for the physical environment, for supplies, and for accessories. Some policy concerning support (software and hardware) should be in place. In implementing any kind of office automation it is important to involve the affected employees at each stage.

In the earlier planning period this has a twofold purpose: to gain acceptance for the project and to obtain additional ideas concerning the way in which any problems might be solved. As implementation proceeds, it will be necessary to provide demonstrations and training for the employees targeted to use the systems. In discussing his experiences at Iowa, Boynton underscored the importance of participation by those concerned, especially in the learning (training) period. The same point was made by Marks at FMC in Kentucky. Without adequate training for appropriate people the machines are not likely to be used well or extensively — at least not at first. And there always will be those who are suspicious of any effort to automate the workplace.

In general, it would appear that most institutions are engaging in the worst kinds of planning or none at all when it comes to microcomputers. Yet the potential uses of micros as well as their current ones could form the foundation for major changes in the way in which we work. Institutional planning should take into consideration not only implementation of aleady ordered machines, but also policies and procedures for deploying new machines. The overriding issue, of course, should be, whether tasks now being accomplished on mainframes (or not being automated at all) can be accomplished as well or better on microcomputers.

If this is the case, then the organization should have a policy and plan for deployment. Unfortunately, this kind of planning requires a level of understanding of micros often not available. In particular, it requires the retraining of systems analysts so that they can be aware of where microcomputing fits into the scheme of things and can be prepared to recommend micros as a better choice than a mainframe.

Earlier chapters implied the desirability of standardizing the microcomputers to be used in an organization. Standardization at all costs is not what is being advocated, because there are a number of very legitimate, specialized uses that might require avoiding standardization. Conversely, however, a policy which generally encourages or requires standardization is probably necessary for the economical and efficient use of resources. When an organization acquires a large number of different kinds of micros, then servicing and programming become major obstacles. Software is not transportable, and quantity purchases of supplies and support services may not be possible. If an organization is deploying micros in a major way, all at one time, standardization will allow the writing of purchase contracts at very favorable prices. Certainly for uses such as those at the University of Iowa's Political Science Department, standardization is mandatory.

MICROCOMPUTER SELECTION AND IMPLEMENTATION

Since little real planning is taking place concerning the deployment of microcomputers, it should not be surprising that there seems to be little concern about the kind or variety of micros being used. With all the apparent benefits of standardization, 52.3 percent (34) of the Dallas survey respondents indicated that there was no attempt to standardize, while 47.7 percent (31) reported that their organizations were trying to impose some form of standardization. Although a majority reported no attempts at standardization, the 47.7 percent which reported some efforts in that direction noted greater concern for deployment planning than was implied by the absence of a general plan for using micros.

Chapter 5 identified some of the factors worth considering when planning for microcomputers. It is clear that few organizations are actually following the rational approach to the implementation of micros suggested earlier. In addition to the general issues discussed earlier, there are also several fundamental issues that should be considered both pre- and post installation. Bruce T. Pace ("Microcomputer Selection and Implementation," *Kilobaud Microcomputing*, March 1981, pp. 120–22) has provided a list of several items in addition to those already discussed. He notes that before work can begin, attention must be paid to electrical work, programming, manuals, supplies, accessories, documentation, procedures development, and other subtle factors. These issues and others are frequently encountered when setting up a large mainframe system, but they are frequently ignored when dealing with microcomputers.

From the Dallas data it is clear that there is some understanding of the problem of hardware and software proliferation. Yet little seems to be being done about it. In the large organizations with several micros, it was typical to have several different makes and models. The most frequently occurring micros were TRS-80 (Models I, II, and III) and Apples. There were, however, significant numbers of other popular micros including Texas Instrument's 99/4, North Star, Cromemco, IBM's 5110 (the survey was run just after IBM's announcement of its personal computer), Commodore, and a potpourri of others. If an organization had two or more micros, as often as not they were of different brands. In essence, implementation of micros in a large organization tends to be haphazard, even when relatively large numbers of the machines are acquired.

THE SUPPORT OF MICROCOMPUTERS

Several of the points noted by Pace concerning preparations for microcomputers revolve around a more general organizational issue: How much hardware and software support is to be provided for any micros acquired? There are several approaches that might be taken in addressing the support issue, and a combination of these approaches is likely the best way to proceed (it is also likely to be the way in which organizations actually behave). First, the micros might be acquired with no formal support. User departments might be forced to find their own servicing and do their own programming. Second, the data processing department might provide some limited programming support. Third, maintenance of hardware and installation of software might be provided centrally on the assumption that most software will be purchased "off-the-shelf."

The level of support provided by the organization is probably indicative of its institutional commitment to the use of microcomputers. In an attempt to assess the directions concerning support for microcomputing, the Dallas survey respondents were asked, "What support does your data processing group provide for microcomputers?" and "Does your organization have one or more programmers assigned for the support of microcomputers?" Of the large organizations using microcomputers, 28.6 percent of the respondents answered "full" support with at least one part-time programmer assigned to micros. By way of contrast, 34.6 percent indicated that something less than full support was offered and no programmers were regularly assigned. On a broader scale, however, 46.9 percent indicated that their organization did provide full support even though specific programmers were not assigned.

One very large firm—one which had a corporate deployment policy with 500 plus microcomputers (that is personal computers rather than process control systems) in place—has established a personal computer fanout organization designed to assist internal users with micros. At FMC in

Kentucky, one of our case study organizations, one progammer devotes a high percentage of his time to the support of microcomputers.

The point of this discussion is that while many organizations are doing little if any real planning for microcomputing, the proliferation of micros is providing substantial support for thier use. Certainly, if microcomputers are to be used effectively, institutional support is required. But when an individual acquires a micro that sits day after day on his/her desk, it is likely that knowledge of at least elementary programming will expand markedly. Some divisions within an organization, especially research and engineering, are likely to be first among those users to do considerable programming without recourse to central data processing services. On the other hand, there are many environments within any organization which would not expect to pick up programming quickly. Expanded internal training programs, which would include an introduction to programming micros, might be a useful adjunct to microcomputer deployment.

IS THE "REAL" WORLD FOR REAL?

Certainly there are a number of very interesting things going on in the use of microcomputers. This chapter showed, through survey results from Dallas and with two specific case studies, some of things large organizations are doing with micros. Certainly from that perspective large organizations are beginning to cope with a changing technology. On the other hand, when we look at the not-very-systematic manner in which large organizations are planning for the uses of micros, there is room for considerable improvement. Once having used microcomputers, few are willing to abandon them. At the University of Iowa and at FMC those using micros gave a clear vote of approval.

In an effort to assess attitudes toward micros on a somewhat broader scale, I asked the Dallas respondents to rate their own personal attitudes toward the use of microcomputers in their own organizations. The rating was done on a scale extending from "1" (meaning "enthusiastic" endorsement) to 5 (meaning "do not see any need for microcomputers"). About 80.6 percent of the large organization users having micros rated themselves as either enthusiastic (41.8 percent) or positive (38.8 percent). Clearly, to know a micro is to respect it.

The purpose of this chapter has been to demonstrate the variety of uses to which micros are actually being put in large organizations. It is clear that much of the marketing effort in corporations like Radio Shack and IBM and Apple will continue to be directed toward the use of microcomputers in large organizations. Early in the book it was noted that one of the major uses to which micros would be put would be as part of distributed processing systems. Here many micros are linked together in relatively large networks of either micros and their peripherals or with large mainframes. While several of the respondents in the Dallas survey indicated that such networks were an objective, not one suggested such a system had already been established.

It appears that, at least among those surveyed, the maximum value is not being extracted from the microcomputers on hand. This, along with the slowness in implementing networking, results from a clearly evident lack of planning. Without appropriate planning—with imagination, intuition, and foresight—not only microcomputers but other technologies designed to improve the work place will not be implemented well. The final chapter will take a look at where the development of microcomputers may lead through the 1990s. The use of various computer technologies is not without cost, but considering the improvements in productivity computers have provided in the past, one can at least imagine that newly developing technologies will provide even greater opportunities.

The Future
of Microcomputers

This book has presented not only state-of-the-art microcomputing as it existed in the early 1980s, but also has looked ahead to what the opportunities will be in the use of microcomputers into the 1990s. This final chapter represents a more self-conscious effort to place the topics presented in the context of the future. An often-asked question when computing equipment is being considered is "Will it be obsolete in two or three years?" Given the present state of technological development, the answer always must be "Yes." For a large organization (or a small one or an individual) the question is inappropriate. Rather, the question should be "Will I get two or three years (or more) worth of real work out of whatever system I acquire?" The answer to this question also can be an emphatic "Yes!" The purpose of this chapter is (1) to provide a peek into what we might expect from computing in the foreseeable future and (2) to provide some assurance that whatever is acquired now can give years of service.

Before going further, however, we will summarize what has been said concerning microcomputers in large organizations. Such organizations clearly are being targeted by micro manufacturers as major markets during the 1980s. Microcomputers can play an important role in the overall information processing needs of large organizations. In order to do so it will be necessary for large organizations to place micros squarely within overall planning for meeting computing and communications needs. Among these needs will be improvement of productivity in the office generally and of management personnel in particular. One of the primary uses to which micros can be put, therefore, is as a manager's work station. Such work stations will provide for word processing, data management, planning and modeling, budgeting, and communications. They can be designed with the software and microcomputers available at the time and will become more sophisticated with advancements in technology. In order to make the maximum use of the technology, however, large organizations will have to plan competently for the deployment of micros, an activity which was clearly neglected during the early 1980s. Finally, micros provide an opportunity for the expansion of creativity in the workplace that has few historical parallels. But where do we go from here?

There are three specific areas, each of which interacts with the others, that are important for us to understand in terms of future directions: (1) the ongoing impact of microcomputing specifically (and computing generally) on our social and organizational lives, (2) hardware futures, and (3) software futures. In each of these areas we will briefly recapitulate the situation as it existed in the early 1980s and then develop forecasts for the future. The forecasts are largely nonquantitative in form and are in part structured as scenarios. Other potential scenarios are possible, of course, and those presented tend toward the most optimistic. Although forecasting is fraught with many problems, we will attempt to peer into the future on the premise that an informed estimate is better than nothing at all.

By the early 1980s it was commonplace to compare the impact of computers on society to the Industrial Revolution of the eighteenth and nineteenth centuries. The suggestions that computers ushered in a second industrial revolution misses the central strengths of computing and why it became the central technology of the final quarter of the twentieth century. (A better and more direct historical analogy is the introduction of movable type (by Gutenberg) during the latter part of the fifteenth century). Within a relatively short period of time (less than twenty years) government, education, business, and religion were undergoing a major revolution — a revolution in the way in which information was processed.

Since the introduction of computers in the 1950s, along with the widespread use of television, we have come to talk about an information overload. Especially in the workplace we have started to obtain volumes of information about all sorts of things. This tendency is continuing. With the introduction of microcomputers and the uniting of computer and television technology, it has become possible on a mass scale to start being more selective about the information we obtain. It is the application of computer technology for assistance in information processing that will become the basis for a new industrial revolution, but this is not the revolution itself.

Back in the early nineteenth century, when Charles Babbage first conceived of the stored program computer, he was not able to consummate his work due in large part to a lack of funding. Government (both the United States and Great Britain) failed to fund Babbage because it did not see the need for a computer. Indeed, the need for a new level of information processing probably did not exist at the time simply because the industrialized nations were just beginning to digest the first industrial revolution and its consequences. It is interesting to speculate on what our society would have been like had Babbage actually built his machine. In all likelihood the impact would not have been as dramatic then as it has been in the twentieth century simply because other elements of society were not producing sufficient information to require organization by machines. Indeed, scientific theories had not yet evolved that would later provide the foundations for adequate use of computing in a technological civilization. In order to understand where we are going with computer technology and what its impact is, we will review the relevant hardware trends, move to software, and then to the organizational implications of these developments.

HARDWARE TRENDS

Table 1 provides a summary of current directions and estimates of where we are likely to be headed into the nineties. (Take a close look at the table, and then return to the discussion.) The table does not include all the hardware available, but only those items likely to make an obvious impact on the use of microcomputers over the period. The entries in the table are placed at the time period when the item is likely to be commercially successful as a part of a finished product available on a widespread basis at moderate to low cost.

TABLE 1. Hardware Trends

	EARLY EIGHTIES	MID-EIGHTIES	LATE EIGHTIES	NINETIES
Microprocessor Chips				
	8-bit processors std.	16-bit processors std.		32-bit processors std.
	64Kbyte memory std.	256K-1M std.		Over 1M std.
	Slow cycle time	Moderate cycle time		Fast cycle time
Communications				
	Asychronous std.	Async/bisync std.		
	Tel. tech. std.	CATV tech. std.	Opt. Fiber intro.	Opt. Fiber std.
	Exper. use of FM	FM Data broadcasts		
Input/Output Devices				
	Typewriter Keyboards			
	Magnetic disks			
	R/O video disk*	R/O video std.	R/W video intro.	R/W video s
	Audio R/W lo**	Audio R/W mod	Audio R/W hi	

  * R/O = Read/Only; R/W = Read/Write
** Audio (voice) Read/Write (input and output) low

Microprocessor Chips

Although the so-called 8-bit central processing units were standard through the early 1980s, it was apparent even by 1982 that the 16-bit CPUs were likely to become the standard—perhaps as early as 1983. Intel was manufacturing a 32-bit processor (the iAPX 432) in 1982 that promised many new opportunities for the late 1980s. The significance of the 8/16/32-bit architecture is twofold: cycle speed and memory address capacity. The 8-bit processors, as noted in Table 1, are relatively slow and can directly address only 64K bytes (K equals 1024 bytes or alphanumeric characters) of memory. The 16-bit processors are faster and can address (depending on the architecture) 256K bytes or more. And the 32-bit processors are very fast with the capability of addressing at least a megabyte (1 million bytes) of memory or, depending on the architecture, perhaps as much as a gigabyte (1 billion bytes) of memory (compare Terry Benson, "The Next Generation—32-bit Microprocessors," *Interface Age*, December 1981, pp. 92–93). The iAPX from Intel illustrated some of the technological problems to be overcome, however, in that it dissipated about 2.5 watts (an 8-bit processor dissipated less than half that), a factor which would determine some physical design characteristics of any housing (including size) needed for a finished system.

Communications

While most complete microprocessor systems of the early 1980s included asynchronous communications as standard, by the mid-1980s synchronous communications were added as a standard feature. The improved speed of the micros using 16-bit processors increased the speed of both forms of communications: in excess of 1200 baud—something rarely possible on general-purpose 8-bit machines. The most nearly standard technique for communications through the early 1980s can be called (for want of a better term) "telephone technology." Part of the reason for this was simply the availability of that technology as compared with others. By the mid-1980s communications in large organizations and at a community level is likely to move toward the large-scale use of cable television (CATV) systems. During that period advances will be made in the use of optical fibers for data transferral. Except for point-to-point communications, optical fiber technology probably will not come into its own as a basis for networking until the early 1990s, however. Experimental use of FM radio broadcasting of machine-readable data was carried on in the early 1980s with widespread use of the medium possible by the mid-1980s.

Input/Output Devices

Data input/output devices also will receive considerable attention during the entire period, although the standard typewriter-like keyboard will continue to be widespread well into the 1990s. The cost of data storage will continue to drop as advances are made in disk storage devices, first with the floppy disk and the Winchester hard disk. By the mid-1980s the prices of the hard disks will have dropped sufficiently to consider them mass-market devices. The most exciting technology was just beginning to be used by the early 1980s: the laser video disk. An earlier device—bubble memories—which promised (at the close of the 1970s) large-scale, low-cost data storage, was aborted by the failure of manufacturers to find an appropriate production/cost reduction ratio. All but one American company (out of four or five) had discontinued manufacture of bubble memory by 1982.

At least one Japanese manufacturer had demonstrated a video disk with both read and write (R/W) capabilities and read-only (R/O) video disk interfaces were being marketed by early 1982. Some video disks contain as much as a gigabyte of data (as compared with about 184,320 bytes for a single-sided, double-density, 40-track, 5.25-inch, floppy disk or 5 to 40 megabytes for a Winchester). A standard, double-spaced, typed page contains about 1500 characters. Consequently, an average floppy disk can hold about 120 typed pages; a 5-megabyte Winchester, about 3333 pages; and a video disk, perhaps as much as 666,666 pages. The latter figure would translate into several hundred books. Moreover, the cost of having video disks duplicated on a small scale, while requiring a specialized laboratory, was relatively small even by the early 1980s. Clearly it would be possible to duplicate entire libraries using video disk technologies.

One of the major innovations likely to become a reality during the 1980s is the increased use of audio input and output: We will be able to enter a considerable amount of data verbally and to extract data in a sound form. The basic technology already was available by the early 1980s, although in a relatively crude form. In fact, the most widespread use of sophisticated audio devices were in toys—not in business environments. Considerable research activity by both American and Japanese computer manufacturers with voice input and output was reported by the trade press early in the decade. Like many other innovations, audio input and output can be most effective with machines that are faster and have larger capacities than those supported by 8-bit processors. Consequently, we should see many additional and highly innovative peripheral devices made available for micros.

By the late eighties or early nineties it will be possible to have a microcomputer on one's desk with capabilities beyond the mainframe computers of only a few years before. The horizons opened by these developments will make access to information available on a scale never before possible. In principle, at least, it should be technologically possible to simply order up a copy of all the works in the Library of Congress (or significant portions thereof) and to house it in a relatively small space. If software developments keep up with the hardware, the possibilities for not only large (and small) organizations but for society as a whole are limitless.

SOFTWARE TRENDS

Across the computer industry, software engineering generally has failed to keep pace with hardware developments. There are a number of reasons for this situation, but at least one is the fact that among large organizations especially, the investment in software is so large that large-scale changes are too costly. The situation is somewhat different with microcomputers, although over time that, too, may change. The advent of micro has spawned a new cottage industry in that it is possible for a few individuals with a micro to make a living by writing programs and offering them for sale. This has led to many poor-to-moderate programs on the market, but it also has led to some very innovative and excellent software at moderate prices. Table 2 reflects the software situation in as much as no dramatic leaps are implied as was true of hardware. Incremental improvement is the likely course of software development.

TABLE 2. Software Trends

	EARLY EIGHTIES	MID-EIGHTIES	LATE EIGHTIES	NINETIES
Languages				
Pascal				
BASIC				
FORTRAN				
COBOL				
Other		Natural languages		
Office Productivity Tools				
Word Processing	Improved	Improved	Improved	
Communications	Improved	Improved	Improved	
Modeling Software	Improved	Improved	Improved	
Data Base	Improved	Improved	Improved	
Instructional Tools				
Comp. Assist. Inst.	Improved	Improved	Improved	
PILOT				
LOGO				
Other				
User Friendly	Improved	Improved	Improved	
Moderate quality	Improved	Improved	Improved	

Programming Languages

Although the death of the standard programming languages, such as COBOL and FORTRAN, have been sounded periodically for 20 years, they are with us yet—and are likely to stay for another 20 years. The reason is largely economic. The investment in programming in these languages is so great that even if some other computer language should gain acceptance, it will be many years before the established languages can be phased out. An example of a language that never quite made it was IBM's PL/I, which was touted as a combination of FORTRAN and COBOL. Even with IBM's strong backing, PL/I was never widely accepted, even by IBM users.

The programming language that was rapidly developing a considerable following by the early 1980s was Pascal (named after the French philosopher Blaise Pascal of the seventeenth century). The U.S. Department of Defense issued an edict that future programming would be done in Ada (named after Babbage's friend and chronicler Ada, the Countess of Lovelace), yet not fully defined by the early 1980s. Even when Ada

151

becomes an operational language, the DOD will not apply it retroactively to the large investment already made largely in COBOL programming. As an easily used language for microcomputers, and for economic reasons as well, BASIC is likely to persist as a widely used language well into the 1990s.

Although there are large numbers of little used programming languages, perhaps the most exciting possibilities revolve around research taking place with the use of natural languages (such as English) as programming tools. The use of natural languages to program computers has been predicted for many years, and although significant efforts have been made to develop natural language techniques, the possibility was still somewhat remote in the early 1980s. It is possible, however, that sufficient progress will be made so that natural language programming will soon become a reality. Natural language programming will initially require the use of very large and fast machines—larger and faster than the capabilities of microcomputers.

But with the advent of the 32-bit CPU, the speed and capacity of microcomputers by the end of the 1980s may well be able to cope with natural language programming. Furthermore, such programming coupled with audio input and output hardware could make traditional programming and programmers obsolete. In a natural language system it would be necessary only to tell the computer, perhaps in a structured manner, what we wanted it to do in order for it to accomplish some task. As audio input/output devices improve it will become possible to do such programming verbally. The potentials for such a system are truly awesome. As is indicated in Table 2, it is possible that we will see some natural language systems within a decade.

Office Productivity Tools

Continuing improvement should take place over the period in the design of applications that fall in the general area of office productivity tools. The improvements will go hand-in-hand with advancements in hardware, because the effectiveness of the programs is to a large extent dependent on the quality of the hardware. These tools include word processing (WP) systems, communications packages, modeling programs, and data base management software. In the case of data base management programs, especially retrieval systems, improvement is mandatory as high-speed, random access systems like laser video disks come to be used as information storage media. The higher speeds of 16-bit and 32-bit processors will allow rapid access of data in larger memories, but fast, random access secondary storage devices also are necessary for such use.

Even if natural language programming does not become available during the time period forecasted, certainly data base systems that use some sort of natural language instruction will become common. By the end of the 1980s, therefore, it should be possible to acquire, at reasonable cost, easily used retrieval programs which are capable of being instructed in simple English phrases and which will be able to access the data contained on video disks. The availability of large quantities of information, capable of rapid retrieval, will be exceedingly helpful not only to business and government but also to researchers. The scientific disciplines should benefit greatly as well as the more traditional disciplines. Historians of the late 1980s should be able to acquire on a laser video disk an entire corpus (perhaps entire centuries of written material), and then, using a desktop computer and a simple retrieval program, extract information in a way never possible before.

Instructional Tools

Instructional techniques within organizations as well as in the commuity at large will change as computer-assisted instruction techniques capitalize on new hardware technologies. With the use of video disks as storage media, the disk can contain not only computer programs and traditional data, but also pictures (both still and moving) and text that can be displayed on the computer's terminal allowing for a level of interactive instruction not possible in the early 1980s. The ability to build interactive instructional systems will be made easier by author languages such as PILOT and its successors, modified or designed to use not only textual but visual and audio information, all of which is stored on a laser disk. Languages such as LOGO will allow more people to learn the rudiments of computer programming. The point is that when there is a microcomputer on the desk of every white-collar worker, everyone ultimately will become a programmer. Creative possibilities will expand with the newer technology as interactive functioning comes from its first experimental roots to full fruition in the late 1980s.

Other Software Trends

Underlying a great many of the software improvements into the 1990s will be the concern of engineers and common programmers for improving the "user friendliness" of the software systems. The key to mass use of computer technology is the ability to make computers easy to use by people who are unwilling or unable to become traditional programmers. Just as the availability of relatively cheap books led to greater literacy (because people had to come to terms with the new technology), so we will see an expansion of computer literacy, although during the early 1980s it was unclear precisely what was meant by such literacy. By that time at least three technologies had swept the world and in the process had changed it: printing, radio/television, and computers.

Printing made possible the modern world, both politically and economically, by making large amounts of information available at a low cost. Radio/television expanded on the dreams and aspirations promoted in print and added an emotional dimension hardly possible with print. Computers by the early 1980s were becoming the third dominant force in information dissemination, and with the ability to combine radio/video and computer technologies, the potentials for growth expanded enormously. It is likely that by the late 1980s every television set will be equipped as an interactive device with a means for two-way communications—a wedding of the television and computing industries making not only expanded productivity tools available to large organizations, but also providing ways for expanding the mind. The twentieth century is already being called the "Information Age."

Finally, over the 1980s we should see an improvement in the quality of the software being produced for all markets. Part of this improved quality should result as a by-product of better tools for traditional (and professional) programmers. Word processing often improves the writing skills of people using such systems. The reason for this is that all of us are willing to spend some additional time on the craft of writing when a computer can generate new copies—something we would not or could not do if we, or a secretary, had to do the typing. The expenditures in time and money are too great when much of the production is by hand. For the same or similar reasons, as program development tools become better (and the tools available on micros, even during the early 1980s, were often superior to those on large mainframes), programmers will be able to craft their programs better. With the advent of the 16-bit and 32-bit microprocessors it certainly will be possible for programmers in a large system environment to do much, if not most, of their development offline on a desk top unit. Thus the inhibitions often placed on programmers to minimize testing time will diminish. And on the micros themselves it will be possible for the same programmers to devote more creative time to new and better programs for use in business, industry, and government.

The future success of microcomputers will depend on the availability of good software which will capitalize on the improvements in hardware. Unlike large, central, mainframe computers, which are supported by a staff of professional programmers, the owner of a personal computer is often in a situation (no matter how much the system is being supported by a central staff) where no programming support is available. Consequently, languages that more nearly approximate English (or French or German or Japanese, or whatever) will become much more important as microcomputers are more widely deployed.

In the absence of programming languages based on natural languages, software systems that provide a reasonable facsimile of natural language interaction will become important. The point is, people who do not have high computer skills will be using the machines. If user-friendly languages and systems are not available, the machines will not be used—or will not be used adequately. While we can expect users to become more computer literate, we cannot expect them to become experts in computer use. Just as most people in a technological society are literate, not all, by any means, are writers.

The developments in hardware and software and the widespread deployment of the products based on those developments will profoundly affect the way we work and play. Some of the trends in social and organizational change are discussed in the next section. Suffice it to say that while the opportunities will be great, there will be problems associated with these developments as well. That the opportunities greatly outnumber the problems has been implied throughout this book. Let us turn then to a discussion of the opportunities and at least some of the problems.

ORGANIZATIONAL IMPACT OF MICROCOMPUTERS

The extended use of high performance microcomputers by the end of the 1980s will contribute to major changes in the way large organizations function. For that matter, before then we will see many changes in the way the population at large works and plays, in part as a result of a closer association of computers and people. Some of these changes will be benign and beneficial—others will be problematic and controversial. The people who can embrace the new technologies and use them effectively will be those in business, industry, government, and education who will continue to make an impact on their organizations. Those who cannot or will not accept change will inevitably be left behind.

One of the reasons computing and computers have been eyed with alarm by some is that from the very beginning the technology and those who served it have been seen as agents of change. Certainly those of us who are part of large organizations have had our lives changed by the advent of computing. And the rate of change is not slowing—in fact, it is increasing. While organizations cannot typically keep up with the rate of change in technology (due to cost, psychology, and social inertia), the fact that technological change rises in an exponential growth pattern forces organizations to come along, even if they do so reluctantly. Every organization possesses its share (sometimes more than its share) of people with a vision of the future so limited that it becomes difficult or impossible to achieve orderly progress.

Role Changes in the Workplace

There are many areas where computing has engendered organizational change, and there are others that will be impacted by the introduction of microcomputers. Two obvious areas will be in role changes in the workplace and in behavior related to the production and uses of information. Some (though by no means all) of these issues are summarized in Table 3. The actual rate at which changes take place in these areas, of course will depend on how systematically and extensively micros are put to use in large organizations. Moreover, the changes noted also will be somewhat dependent on the ability of vendors and internal programming staffs to produce appropriate software that will keep up with hardware capabilities. Change is, like death and taxes, inevitable. Whether change is helpful and positive or whether it has a negative impact is a function of how well we can respond to changing technological conditions and opportunities.

TABLE 3. Organizational Impact

EARLY EIGHTIES	MID-EIGHTIES	LATE EIGHTIES	NINETIES
Role Changes in the Workplace			
Hi paper dep.*	Mod paper dep.	Mod paper dep.	Lo paper dep.
Hi clerical**	Mod clerical	Mod clerical	Low clerical
Lo Mgt. Use***	Mod Mgt. Use	Mod Mgt. Use	Hi Mgt. Use
Home wk lo****	Home wk mod	Home wk mod	Home wk hi
Information Access and Exchange			
Limited Elec Mail	Expanded Elec Mail	Most mail elec	All mail elec
Comp/elec conf lo†	Comp/elec conf mod/	Comp/elec conf mod	Comp/elec conf hi
Group plan lo‡	Group plan better	Group plan better	Group plan better
Org news low†‡	Org news mod	Org news mod	Org news hi
Info access lo‡‡	Info access mod	Info access mod	Info access hi

```
          * High paper dependence (memos, reports, etc.)
         ** High clerical personnel investment
        *** Low direct management use of computers
       **** Work from home low
          † Use of Computer/electronic conferencing low
          ‡ Group planning for organizational objectives low
         †‡ Level of intra-organizational news low
         ‡‡ Inadequate information access for decision-making
```

Perhaps the first change we are likely to see, and one which most of us will approve of, is decreasing dependence on paper: paper memoranda, paper reports, and the like. By the 1990s the excessive dependence of most large organizations on paper of various sorts will have diminshed to a large extent. The reasons for decreasing dependence on paper include the steeply rising cost of paper itself. Along with the growing cost of paper has been a steep rise in the number of reports the average manager must at least glance at and sometimes assimilate. As computers make it easier to produce larger and more comprehensive reports, it is likely that the amount of time spent with numerous individual reports will decline. Thus, at a time when better, more accurate, and more timely data are available to serve as a basis for decision-making, specific items of information will receive less attention.

Both microcomputers and large mainframes can assist accessibility by allowing us to make more intelligent and selective use of the information produced. In order to accomplish this effectively, however, we will have to forego a tendency to want to access hard copy. As the price per character of storage (both main memory and peripherals such as magnetic and laser disks) continues to fall, so will the ability to acquire easy access to information as needs increase, thus allowing us to pay attention to those items we need.

The result of lower levels of physical paper pushing will lead to a reduced need for traditional clerical support. This does not mean, necessarily, that organizations will have fewer secretaries, but these people will become more productive contributors to organizational needs and objectives. In fact, it was only during the twentieth century that secretaries came to be viewed largely as clerical employees—a development consistent with greater dependence on printed matter (it had to be produced and put somewhere). In the previous century secretaries were viewed as highly placed people assisting in the decision-making process of large organizations, acting as scribes and archivists for those with central decision-making responsibilities. With the advent of word processing, electronic mail, and online access to information, the tasks of filing and handling paper will be minimal.

My own experience provides an example of the progression. Early in my career, before I had sufficient need to have a secretary, I did almost all my own writing and typing of memos, manuscripts, and the like. As time progressed, I acquired a secretary but still continued to do the writing (usually with a typewriter but sometimes with a pencil and paper) while my secretary did the final preparation and distribution of manuscripts. When access to word processing became available, I found that I could work as easily at a terminal as I could at a typewriter. The result of this was that the secretary was no longer needed to type version after version of something—the computer did it all. With the acquisition of a microcomputer with word processing capabilties it became possible to do writing at home (or almost anywhere) while only uploading to the large machine when necessary. The secretary's time was freed for more productive, creative, and responsible work. On top of that, because I could make minor changes easily, my writing tended to improve.

For some managers and other professionals the most difficult issue to confront is the potential change in their own work habits. When a micro-computer-based work station is available to them, a mild crisis may occur. Under the operating conditions of the early 1980s, except for selected industries, most middle to upper level managers (as well as various professionals such as university faculty members) used clerical and secretarial services, especially for word processing. In a technological period when that is no longer necessary, the status that accrues to an individual with a secretary will no longer be available.

When a memorandum or letter moves directly from one microcom-puter to another with electronic mail, another secretarial function will have fallen by the wayside. It will mean that many managers and profes-sionals who do not now type will have to learn. The point is that direct management use of terminals and micros will increase from a relatively low rate to a very high rate. The inability to cope with this change in style sooner or later will lead to reduced promotional opportunities and reduced visibility within the organization (or perhaps to an undesirable kind of visibility).

One of the most impressive opportunities large organizations will have presented to them through the use of microcomputers in conjunction with greatly improved systems of communications and networking will be the ability to distribute work geographically. For some organizations it even may be possible to do away with a significant amount of physical plant. Although professionals and managers always have done a certain amount of work at home, it has tended to be work which only they, as indi-viduals, could do or work which required little direct organizational sup-port. No longer will work-at-home possibilities be limited to these restricted applications. In a computing environment, where the manager has a work station at home and high-speed communications (perhaps through the lo-cal cable television system, ultimately interfaced to a regional or national packet switched network) are available, much if not most traditional work can be accomplished without ever leaving the home. Through networking it even might be possible to make management techniques such as matrix management work effectively with people conferencing (from home) by computer and video techniques. Opportunities to distribute the workplace will be enormous.

Information Access and Exchange

Among the primary reasons the behavioral changes noted above will take place is the changing way in which we will generate, access, and exchange information. In earlier chapters we discussed the technological bases for new opportunities in the areas of information access and exchange, and some review is desirable as a way of indicating the direction in which the world is moving. One of the best examples of the technology is electronic mail. Clearly it is less expensive to use an electronic mail system than to use more traditional mail techniques. Within an organization it may be as much as 230 percent less costly to use electronic mail than traditional mail.

Moreover, by the end of the 1980s considerable national and international mail also will be carried electronically. Even in the early 1980s it was possible for an individual to establish an account with Western Union, access Western Union's system with a microcomputer or a terminal, type in a letter (Mail-Gram), and have it delivered the next day. For many organizations this approach became cost-effective as personnel and mailing costs increased. By the early 1990s electronic mail will be the standard mode of communication within large organizations. The electronic mail system may be an incremental add-on cost to a large centralized system (as it was in the late 1970s for Texas Instruments) or it may be a distributed mail system in a large local-area network. In any event, cost alone will dictate that we use such systems.

Some large organizations already use "teleconferencing," meaning either audio conferencing by telephone or video conferencing if the organization has a sufficient video and voice capability. But the entire process can be made more effective and efficient through a wedding of computer and information storage and retrieval. Conferencing systems ultimately will allow a level of interaction impossible to obtain with other technologies simply because of the cost of personnel and travel. As energy costs increase, large organizations will come to make better use of the twin technologies of video and computing.

By the late 1980s most manager's work stations will be integrated computer/video systems (as will most home television sets), allowing for two-way communications at almost any level the organization requires. This capability in turn will allow for more varied and detailed group planning activities. In a highly technological society, planning is an essential activity if an organization is to stay competitive and vital—if it is to carry out its mission whether in the public or private sectors. Through widely deployed conferencing systems it should be possible, using updated (and automated) techniques such as the Delphi Method (a "soft" forecasting technique based on consensual information from experts) and modeling of various sorts, to do planning on a scale never before envisioned.

Finally, in an expanded electronic environment we will see a move from low levels of information access to much higher levels into the 1990s. The information referred to here is the kind that can make the organization work more effectively in a variety of ways. When managers can actually access required information for making decisions, then decisions will be better informed. When all employees can be kept better informed concerning the work and objectives of the organization, in an ongoing and timely fashion, worker satisfaction is likely to rise. Many organizations in the early 1980s published newsletters and memos, and in many organizations there were multiple information sheets from many different departments. One of the difficulties of such a situation is that many people are involved in doing that kind of intraorganizational activity and many people are receiving information they do not need or desire. In an electronic environment, using a local version of electronic newspapers, a more selective (yet at the same time a more timely) approach to information dissemination is possible. Furthermore, with electronic systems of distribution to local work stations, printing and paper costs can be reduced. In a completely distributed local network environment it would be necessary to commit only one low-cost microcomputer to such a task, and yet have it accessible by everyone. In a larger, more centralized environment, similar systems can be envisioned.

CONCLUDING OBSERVATIONS

Change is taking place in large organizations. Over the next two decades the pace of change will accelerate because the pace of computer-related technological innovation is accelerating. The changes that will take place should not be viewed with fear or apprehension unless, of course, one fails to prepare for and deal with those changes. A great many beneficial changes will come as a by-product of microcomputer technology. By the end of the decade micros will be everywhere, whether we know it or not. Refrigerators and ovens and copying machines, controlled by microcomputers, will all be talking to us soon. Much of our entertainment and information will take place through microcomputers or with a combination of microcomputer and television technology. The same technology with which we shall have to deal on a personal level also will be making major inroads in the workplace—it already is, although most large organizations apparently would rather not confront the issue.

Real (rational) planning for microcomputing does not appear to be available in most large organizations and, at least on the part of some, there is active hostility. Yet microcomputers are coming whether we have a negative or positive view. And the fact of the matter is that most people that know about them in large organizations will come to have a highly positive view. The question is, then, "What is an appropriate organizational response to microcomputing, and how shall it be integrated into the overall information processing needs of the organization?" The best way to confront the problem is to recognize that microcomputers can be a major aid in producing greater productivity at the managerial level and among white-collar workers in general.

Another major technological issue that large organizations will have to face involves communications. The two technologies are bound together in that microprocessors will run intelligent copiers and recording devices as well as being the basis for a manager's work station. Moreover, in local area networks the intelligence of the network is often completely distributed — a concept difficult for people trained in a large centralized system to understand. Down to the level of the modem which connects a microcomputer or terminal into the communications network, there is intelligence in that the modem itself will contain a microprocessor, frequently the same one as that in the manager's work station.

The next major area of expansion in the use of microcomputers is with large organizations. The vendors and manufacturers of the machines are convinced of this. The new communications technologies will make truly distributed processing systems possible at reasonable costs. In areas of office automation the micro will become the fundamental building block. And a manager's work station was possible to put into effect even in the early 1980s. It was clear that many large organizations were already doing innovative things with microcomputers and that a few had progressed in a major way (although these were often high technology companies themselves).

Organizational planners are concerned about two issues: Should they wait a year or two for better technology, and how soon will anything they buy now become obsolete? The answer to the former question is that it will not help to wait a year or two. By that time there will be even more technological innovations. The decision will be just as difficult then as today. In answer to the second part of the question, whatever is bought today is likely to be technologically obsolete in a year or less. But purchasing procedures in large organizations will never be fast enough to keep up with technological growth. This year's microcomputer will be just as useful next year as it is this year. Consequently, if planning is based on functionality, then it should be possible to begin deploying micros instantly, and yet avoid at least some of the consequences of obsolesence. From a financial perspective, however, it probably would be well to amortize the machines over a relatively short period of time (say three years), because the pressure for newer devices will tend to accumulate.

Should one wait to buy equipment because prices are dropping? The answer is "No." The real prices of microcomputers are, in fact, dropping. What is happening, however, is much the same as with mainframe computers. The manufacturers hit a pricing level by 1982 which was apt to remain fairly constant for a total system (ranging between about $3000 and $8000, depending on the precise mix of devices acquired) for some time, although they were providing considerably improved function. One example is the price of memory. Memory chips, by 1982, had fallen in price to a point where manufacturers could just about give memory away. Consequently, any machine beyond $2500 (and many below that price) was equipped with as much memory as it could handle at the time of sale (for 8-bit machines this meant 64K, and for 16-bit machines, 128K). A somewhat equivalent drop in the CPU microprocessor chip also occurred. The result was that many add-ons were becoming standard: magnetic disks, better keyboards, color capabilities, and so forth. That situation is likely to remain in effect through at least the mid-1980s.

Even with the Reagan Administration depression of the early 1980s, however, the boom in the microcomputer business is likely to keep the industry healthy and competitive for years. We should note, however, that the top price of a microcomputer is not likely to rise above about $8000 (although it was tried by a few). This price by 1982 was forcing stand-alone word processors, once in the $15,000-to-$20,000 range, down to more reasonable levels. It also is possible that the price will drop lower as micros become more and more of a mass market product. At competitive prices, the buyer will receive value for any expenditure.

In summary, we can say that into the 1990s micros will help change the face of the workplace. Institutions and organizations can either capitalize on those changes or be dragged along by events. Proper and appropriate implementation and deployment of microcomputers in large organizations will likely occur when they are placed in the total context of planning for computing. They may be used inefficiently and ineffectively when we fail to plan. The use of micros will open up exciting new opportunities for most organizations.

Suggestions
for Further Reading

The reading material presented here includes, but is not limited to, most of the sources used in the preparation of this book. This is not a formal bibliography, but a short bibliographical essay for those wishing to do further reading on microcomputers. Material concerning micros and their uses is being published at such a rapid rate that some of the articles and books listed below may be out-of-date by the time you finish this book. However, if you find your interest in micros has increased through reading this book, then some of the reading suggestions found below will be of assistance. This is not a complete bibliography, but it should be sufficient to point the way to a better understanding of computing. When preparing the background material for this book, I did a literature search using Dialog, an automated bibliographical service available from Lockheed. Searching between 1977 and 1981 I picked up nearly 10,000 articles on microcomputers/microprocessors, over 2000 on word processing, more than 1700 on microcomputers and distributed data processing. And the data bases did not, apparently, include a number of the magazines referenced below!

The only way to keep up with computing generally, and microcomputing in particular, is to read the extensive periodical literature available. On a relatively light technical level, but most current, are several tabloid newspapers published weekly or biweekly for the computing industry. These include *Computer World, Info World, Computer Business News,* and *Infosystems News. Computer World* is the best established among these newspapers and is the most varied. *Info World* reports microcomputing more extensively than does *ComputerWorld.*

Many of the issues discussed in this book are presented in a number of slick monthly magazines pointed primarily toward management. Examples of such general computing publications are *Datamation, Infosystems,* and *Computer Decisions.* Problems concerning communications and networks are discussed in *Telecommunications* and *Data Communications.* The entire area of office automation is covered by *Office Automation* and *The Office.* These publications frequently are available without charge to management personnel and are worth purusing. These journals are especially useful for those with a desire to keep abreast of developing technology and its impact on management.

It is impossible to monitor microcomputing without reading at least some of the magazines now available that are devoted entirely to micros. Many of these magazines are now routinely available on magazine racks in drug and grocery stores as well as in bookstore chains. These magazines range from the highly technical, hardware-oriented publications to relatively soft, user-oriented, periodicals. Most are somewhere between highly technical and popular. A business and user oriented magazine is *Desktop Computing. Creative Computing, Interface Age,* and *Personal Computing* are all software-oriented, stressing organizational applications and recreational computing. *Microsystems* is an S-100 and CP/M oriented technical publication, while *Datacast* is a CP/M software-oriented magazine providing, among other things, tutorials on specific applications software, such as "Wordstar." *Byte* is a relatively technical publication emphasizing hardware but certainly not restricted to that. *Byte* also is the largest (in terms of the number of pages printed) of the magazines. Two quite good journals are published for users of Radio Shack's TRS-80 series: *80-Microcomputing* and *US 80. Kilobaud Microcomputing* is a general purpose publication, somewhat more technical than *Creative Computing* but somewhat less technical than *Byte.*

A number of publishers have started series aimed at microcomputer users. These books, as well as more general books on computing, can now be found in the "Computer Science" sections of bookstores. Prentice-Hall's Spectrum series is easily available. Another large publisher of technical books is Wiley. A third major publisher of micro books is Osborne/Mc-Graw-Hill, which publishes Adam Osborne's extensive list of books on microcomputing. Several of the microcomputer magazines also have established book publishing arms. A useful introduction to microcomputing is Osborne's series, *An Introduction to Microcomputers.* The first volume (Volume 0) *The Beginner's Book,* is helpful. Other useful introductions include Jules A. Cohen, *How to Computerize your Small Business,* and John M. Nevison, *Executive Computing.*

James Martin has written several standard texts on data communications and network technology, including *Telecommunications and the Computer, Design Strategy for Distributed Data Processing,* and *Teleprocessing Network Organization.* A more popular approach to teleprocessing is Martin's *Telematic Society.* Other introductions to teleprocessing are Cay Weitzman, *Distributed Micro/Minicomputer Systems,* and Trevor Housley, *Data Communications and Teleprocessing Systems.*

To reiterate, this is not a comprehensive bibliography. There are a large number of books and periodicals now being published for those interested in computing. These publications run the gamut from light, popular introductions to highly technical treatments. Information on some of the most current technologies may be available only from manufacturers or from technical scholarly or industry-oriented journals. Most university libraries have extensive publications concerning computing, as do public libraries. Both computer magazines and books can be obtained from virtually any retail computer store. A single source for comparative information concerning both software and hardware is the *Datapro Directory of Small Computers,* published by Datapro Research Corporation and frequently updated.

Glossary

Because some of the terms used in this book may not be familiar to the more casual reader, this short glossary is provided and generally follows definitions given in the text. When there has been some question concerning definition, those given in the glossary for *EDP Solutions* (Datapro Research Corporation) have been followed. While there are several dictionaries of computer terms available, any source more than five years old may not have many currently used terms in it.

ADA — A computer programming language developed for the U.S. Department of Defense and adopted as the standard language by the DOD.

answer modem — See modem.

Apple — A widely marketed, popular, personal computer based on the 8 bit, 6502 microprocessor chip (Apple II).

ASCII — American (National) Standard Code for Information Interchange, X3.4-1968. A 7-bit-plus parity code established by the American National Standards Institute to achieve compatibility among data services and consisting of 96 displayed upper and lower case characters and 32 nondisplayed control codes.

asynchronous transmission — A mode of data communications transmission in which time intervals between transmitted characters may be of unequal length. The transmission is controlled by start and stop elements at the beginning and end of each character; hence it is also called start-stop transmission.

bandwidth — The range of frequencies assigned to a channel or system. The difference expressed in Hertz between the highest and lowest frequencies of a band.

baseband (signaling) — Transmission of a signal at its original frequencies, i.e., unmodulated.

BASIC — Beginner's All-purpose Symbolic Instruction Code. A common, algebra-like, high-level, interactive, computer programming language now common on almost all microcomputers.

batch processing — A technique in which a number of data transactions are collected over a period of time and aggregated for sequential processing.

baud — A unit of transmission speed equal to the number of discrete conditions or signal events per second. Baud is the same as "bits per second" only if each signal event represents exactly one bit, although the two terms are often used interchangeably.

bisynchronous transmission — Binary synchronous (bisync) transmission. Data transmission in which synchronization of characters is controlled by timing signals generated at the sending and receiving stations in contrast to asynchronous transmission.

broadband — A communications channel having a bandwidth characterized by high data transmission speeds (10,000 to 500,000 bits per second). Often used when describing communications systems based on cable television technology.

bus — The organization of electrical paths within a circuit. A specific bus, such as the S-100, provides a standard definition for specific paths.

central processing unit — See CPU.

centralized network — A computer network with a central processing node through which all data and communications flow.

Centronics — A manufacturer of computer printers. Centronics pioneered the use of a parallel interface between printers and computers. That interface, using Centronic standards, is sometimes referred to as a Centronics parallel interface.

COBOL — COmmon Business Oriented Language. A computer language that makes use of English-like statements especially adapted to business uses.

Commodore — A manufacturer of microcomputers including the PET and CBM series.

communications — See data communications. Transmission of intelligence between points of origin and reception without alteration of sequence or structure of the information content.

communications network — The total network of devices and transmission media (radio, cables, etc.) necessary to transmit and receive intelligence.

computer network — One or more computers linked with users or each other via a communications network.

CP/M — Control Program for Microcomputers. Manufactured and marketed by Digital Research, Inc.

CPU — Central Processing Unit. The "brain" of the general purpose computer that controls the interpretation and execution of instructions. The CPU does not include interfaces, main memory, or peripherals.

cursor — A position indicator frequently employed in video (CRT or VDT) output devices or terminals to indicate a character to be corrected or a position in which data is to be entered.

database — A nonredundant collection of interrelated data items processible by one or more applications.

data communications — The transmission and reception of data, often including operations such as coding, decoding, and validation.

data file — A collection of related data records organized in a specific manner. In large systems data files are gradually being replaced by data bases in order to limit redundancy and improve reliability and timeliness.

data management system — A system which provides the necessary procedures and programs to collect, organize, and maintain data files or data bases.

disk storage (sometimes spelled disc storage) — Information recording on continuously rotating magnetic platters. Storage may be either sequential or random access.

distributed data processing (DDP) — An organization of data processing such that both processing and data may be distributed over a number of different machines in one or more locations.

distributed network — A network configuration in which all node pairs are connected either directly or through redundant paths through intermediate nodes.

DOS (Disk Operating System) — A general term for the operating system used on computers using disk drivers. Also see operating system.

download — The ability of a communications device (usually a microcomputer acting as an intelligent terminal) to load data from another device or computer to itself, saving the data on a local disk or tape.

electronic mail — A system to send messages between or among users of a computer network and the programs necessary to support such message transfers.

ETHERNET — A local area network and its associated protocol developed by (but not limited to) Xerox. Ethernet is a baseband system.

floppy disks — Magnetic, low-cost, flexible data disks (or diskettes) usually either 5.25 or 8 inches in diameter.

FORTRAN — FORmula TRANslating system. A common computer language primarily used for scientific, mathematical, and engineering problems.

Hertz — A unit of frequency equal to one cycle per second. Abbreviated as Hz.

IBM — International Business Machines. One of the primary manufacturers of computer (usually though not exclusively large-scale) equipment.

interactive processing — Processing in which transactions are processed one at a time, often eliciting a response from a user before proceding. An interactive system may be conversational, implying continuous dialogue between the user and the system. (Contrast with batch processing.)

interface — A shared boundary between system elements defined by common physical interconnections, signals, and meanings of interchanged signals.

kilohertz — 1000 Hertz. Also see Hertz.

local area network — A computer and communications network which covers a limited geographical area. It allows every node to communicate with every other node and does not require a central node or processor.

logical record — A collection of items independent of their physical environment. Portions of the same logical record may be located in different physical records.

mainframe computer — A large-scale computing system.

manager's work station — A microcomputer containing an integrated package of software designed to improve the productivity of managers. A work station will usually, though not exclusively, include a word processor, a spreadsheet program, a communications program, and a data manager.

menu — A multiple choice list of procedures or programs to be executed.

microcomputer — A computer system of relatively small physical size and, in former times, limited in speed and address capacity. Usually, though not exclusively, a single-user computer.

microprocessor — The central processing unit of a microcomputer which contains the logical elements for manipulating data and performing arithmetic or logic operations on it.

minicomputer — A computer system, usually a time-sharing system, sometimes faster than microcomputers but not as fast as large mainframe computers.

modem — MOdulator/DEModulator. A device which modulates and demodulates signals transmitted over communication facilities. A modem is sometimes called a data set.

network — See communications network and computer network.

node — Any station, terminal, computer, or other device in a computer network.

off-the-shelf — Production items which are available from current stock and need not be either newly purchased or immediately manufactured. The term also relates to computer software or equipment that can be used by customers with little or no adaptation, thereby saving them the time and expense of developing their own.

office automation — Refers to efforts to provide automation for common office tasks including word processing, filing, and record keeping.

OMNINET — A local area network developed by Corvus Systems.

online processing — A general data processing term concerning access to computers, in which the input data enters the computer directly from the point of origin or in which output data is transmitted directly to where it is used.

operating system — A program which manages the hardware and software environment of a computing system.

originate-only-modem — A modem that can originate data communications but cannot answer a call from another device.

Pascal — A structured computer programming language more general in character than either FORTRAN or BASIC but not as verbose as COBOL. Frequently used in microcomputers and minicomputers.

peripheral — Computer equipment external to the CPU and performing a wide variety of input and output functions.

personal computer — An alternative name for microcomputer which suggests that the computer is to be used for individual work production or entertainment.

physical record — A basic unit of data that is read or written by a single input/output command to the computer.

PL/I — Programming Language One. A high-level programming language designed for use in a wide range of commercial and scientific computer applications and often thought of as a combination of FORTRAN and COBOL.

program — A set of instructions in a programming language used to define an operation or set of operations to a computer.

protocol — A formal set of conventions governing the format and relative timing of message exchange in a communications network.

Radio Shack (Tandy) — A consumer electronics manufacturer and major distributor of microcomputers.

RAM — Random Access Memory. Semiconductor memory used in the construction of computers. The time required to obtain data is independent of the location.

ROM — Read-Only-Memory. A memory device used in computers that cannot be altered during normal computer use. Usually a semiconductor device.

remote access — Pertaining to communication with a computer by a terminal distant from the computer.

remote batch terminal (RBT) — A terminal used for entering jobs and data into a computer from a remote site for later batch processing.

remote job entry (RJE) — Input of a batch job from a remote site and receipt of output via a line printer or other device at a remote site.

software — A term used to contrast computer programs with the "iron" or hardware of a computer system.

spreadsheet programs — Computer programs that allow data to be entered as elements of a table or matrix with rows and columns in order to manipulate the data. Programs widely available on microcomputers are VISICALC and SUPERCALC.

start-stop transmission — See asynchronous transmission.

terminal — A device that allows input and output of data to a computer. The term is most frequently used to describe equipment which has a keyboard for data entry and either a printer or a video tube for displaying data.

text editor — A program that provides flexible editing facilities on a computer for the purpose of allowing data entry from a keyboard terminal without regard for the eventual format or medium for publication. With a text editor, data (text, copy, or whatever) can be edited easily and quickly.

text formatter — A program for reading a data file created with a text editor and transforming the raw file into a neatly formatted listing.

transaction processing — A style of data processing in which files are updated and results are generated immediately as a result of data entry.

TRSDOS — The disk operating system supplied with several of the Radio Shack TRS-80 computers.

turnkey system — A system in which the manufacturer or distributor takes full responsibility for complete system design and installation and supplies all necessary hardware, software, and documentation.

upload — Refers to the ability to send data from an originating terminal (usually a microcomputer) to another computer or terminal.

VISICALC — A popular spreadsheet program by Personal Software.

Winchester disks — Hard magnetic disk storage media in sealed containers. (Not all sealed disks are Winchester drives.)

Index